· CONCISE GUIDE TO ·

Nutrition
in the
Horse

David W. Ramey, D.V.M.
and
Stephen E. Duren, Ph.D.

Howell Book House
New York

Also by David W. Ramey, D.V.M.

Horsefeathers: Facts Versus Myths About Your Horse's Health

Concise Guide to Medications and Supplements in the Horse

Concise Guide to Tendon and Ligament Injuries in the Horse

Concise Guide to Navicular Syndrome in the Horse

Concise Guide to Colic in the Horse

Concise Guide to Arthritis in the Horse

The Anatomy of an Horse

Copyright © 1998 by David W. Ramey, D.V.M. and Stephen E. Duren, Ph.D.

Howell Book House
A Simon & Schuster Macmillan Company
1633 Broadway
New York, NY 10019

MACMILLAN is a registered trademark of Macmillan, Inc.

Library of Congress Cataloging-in-Publication
Ramey, David W.
   Concise guide to nutrition in the horse / David W. Ramey and Stephen E. Duren.
    p.   cm.
   Includes index.
   ISBN 0-87605-089-5
   I. Horses--Feeding and feeds.   2. Horses--Nutrition.   I. Duren, Stephen E.   II. Title.
SF285.5.R35   1998
636.1'0852--dc2I   98-5054
                                   CIP

Manufactured in the United States of America

10 9 8 7 6 5 4 3 2

CONTENTS

Acknowledgments　*iv*

Introduction　*v*

1　What's in Feed?　1

2　The Horse's Digestive System　19

3　Feedstuffs　31

4　Making Horse Feed　49

5　Feed Supplements　61

6　The Ground Rules　79

7　Feeding Your Horse for Maintenance　85

8　Feeding for Growth and Reproduction　95

9　Feeding Performance Horses　107

10　Feeding Horses with Disease Conditions　115

11　Feed Myths　131

Epilogue　*145*

Index　*147*

ACKNOWLEDGMENTS

To the best of the authors' knowledge, this book represents the first collaboration between an equine veterinarian and an equine nutritionist who are not the same person. That combination has been educational and entertaining for both of the authors; hopefully you will find the results equally satisfying.

The authors would like to thank Lynda Fenneman who, freed from the constraints of anatomical accuracy, was able to let her imagination run amok and come up with the wonderful illustrations. Dr. Kathleen Crandell was of tremendous help in providing insight and information on nutrition as well as in making sure that the end result was both accurate and enjoyable. Linda Rarey again chipped in with her succinct and cogent comments; her three-line summaries of the books are priceless. Jonna Pangburn Dennis, homeless in Texas, also helped make sure that all this talk about what horses eat was understandable.

Dr. Stephen Duren would like to especially thank his wife Denise, their son Grayson and their daughter Shae for their endless and continuing love and support (which comes regardless of a continuing lack of success in harvesting an elk).

Dr. David Ramey would like to especially thank his wife Elizabeth for her continuing good sense of humor as his typing skills continue to improve. Jackson, who has learned that keyboards are one of life's amusements, has become an occasional, though inadvertent, contributor. Aidan is on the way.

INTRODUCTION

You can omit a lot of the things you do to and for your horse. You can almost certainly forget to buy the spray that helps make your horse's coat shine. You can occasionally forget to clean out his feet. You can be a couple of weeks late on deworming or wait another week before calling your farrier to trim his feet. You cannot, however, *ever* forget to feed your horse (for very long). For your horse's body to work properly, it needs to eat properly.

One of the more common reasons you might own a horse is so it can perform. Performance means competition; competition suggests that winning is important; to win, an "edge" is often looked for. Many horse owners perceive that the "edge" to their horse's winning performance can be provided through proper nutrition. That perception is not entirely incorrect; although proper nutrition won't overcome limitations that are inherent in an individual animal (an individual animal can only do what it can do), there's no question that without proper nutrition, a performance horse won't be able to perform to its capabilities. However, since different horses work in different capacities (pleasure, roping, jumping, dressage, polo, etc.), it should come as no surprise that eating properly may imply different things for different horses.

If you have baby horses, you will undoubtedly want them to grow up big, strong and healthy. That means proper nutrition is important, starting with what you feed the mare that you hope will give you the baby you want. Still another reason you might want to feed your horse properly is that you care about it. Owning a horse is an emotional (as well as financial) investment. It's only natural that you should want to take good care of a good friend. Feeding is a time-honored way to express affection and caring. (Have you ever gone away hungry from your grandmother's house?) It's properly perceived that providing good nutrition is an important way to help take care of your horse.

Unfortunately for the horse owner who wants to provide the "best" feeding program for his or her horse, there is a bewildering array of choices. Depending on the part of the world in which you live, your horse may be provided with feeds and supplements that differ greatly in the composition, quantity and quality of the nutrients they provide. Thus, it's neither possible nor appropriate to recommend one ideal diet for any horse. There is, after all, more than one way to skin a cat.

That being said, feed is pretty predictable stuff. That is, there are only so many things that feed contains. You can vary the *amounts* of stuff in individual feeds or supplements, but all feeds contain essentially the *same* stuff. Thus, it is possible to come up with a diet that is appropriate for your horse, using whatever types of feed are available, as long as you keep in mind what's in the feed you are using.

Think of a motor vehicle. Every single motor vehicle you buy will get you from point "A" to point "B" (hopefully). Thus, when buying a motor vehicle, your choices are for items such as the color you want, the style and the options available. All of your choices may affect the *price* of your motor vehicle; however, all of the motor vehicles from which you are choosing ultimately do the same thing. In that way, buying feed for your horse is just like buying a car. You have only one goal (feeding your horse properly), but you have lots of options from which to choose.

This book is designed to help you understand your goals and choices. It begins by discussing what feed actually provides the horse. Next, the book addresses how horses use their feed. Chapters on feeds that are available for your horse, how feeds are manufactured and on the many types of supplements available for purchase (the car wax and the scented air fresheners of the motor vehicle example) will help you sort through the bewildering array of product options that you are confronted with. The book then presents feeding strategies for horses involved in different activities or at different stages in their life. A discussion of nutrition and how it relates to a number of important diseases of the horse precedes the final chapter, which is a discussion of feed-related myths (of which there are many).

It's a good thing to want to feed your horse properly. Your horse will undoubtedly perform at its best if you can provide it with an optimum feeding program. Feeding a horse properly isn't complicated and it isn't particularly difficult as long as you keep your nutritional goals in mind and understand how to achieve them. In fact, the biggest difficulty in choosing a feed for your horse often arises from trying to distinguish between the many companies and products that are competing for your business. Hopefully, with the help of this book, you will soon be able to do just that.

CHAPTER I

What's in Feed?

E<small>VERY SINGLE THING THAT YOU FEED YOUR HORSE HAS</small> the same stuff in it. Think about it; all feeds, from oat hay to apples, contain the same things, only in different amounts. (There are only so many things that *can* be found in feed.) Feed is merely a package of its component parts.

If you understand what's in feed, the whole idea of feeding your horse becomes a lot more simple and a lot more constructive. Rather than discussing whether particular feeds are "good" or "bad," you can begin to think about the relative merits of each feed. You can begin to make reasonable choices about what you are going to feed your horse and why. You'll probably find that it's a lot more fun and useful to feed your horse with a purpose than it is to worry and wonder about whether one feed is better or worse than the other.

ENERGY

Energy runs the chemical reactions in the horse's body, provides the fuel that allows the heart to beat and the muscles to contract, allows fetuses to develop in mares, provides the milk that allows foals to grow and simulates growth and development in young horses (among other things). Your horse won't be able to jump big fences or ford raging rivers if it doesn't have enough energy in its diet. Something like 80 to 90 percent of the feed that's eaten by horses is used to fulfill their energy requirements. Thus, the main focus of any horse's diet is to make sure that it has enough energy. Energy is measured in units called calories, which is a measurement of the heat produced when you burn food; for all intents and purposes, you can use the terms *energy* and *calories* interchangeably (although a serious nutritionist might take issue with you on this point).

Energy is not a nutrient, however. It is the end product of the digestive breakdown of one of three different components that are found in all feeds: carbohydrates, protein and fat. Each of these components is largely made up of the same chemical elements (carbon, hydrogen and oxygen) so perhaps it's not surprising that the end result of their breakdown (energy) is the same.

Carbohydrates

Carbohydrates (a chemical term referring to the fact that the molecule contains the element carbon and water) are the primary source of energy for any horse. Since horses eat plants, this is inevitable; roughly 75 percent of all plant material is made up of carbohydrates. However, all carbohydrates are not created equal. There are many different kinds of carbohydrates in horse feed. The horse is able to digest and use these different types of carbohydrates to varying degrees (this fact has some important implications in deciding which type of carbohydrate you choose to feed your horse). Carbohydrates can be split into two broad categories: structural and nonstructural.

Structural carbohydrates (also known as *plant fiber*) such as cellulose, hemicellulose and lignin act as the skeleton for the body of a plant.

2

These are tough, rigid compounds: so tough that no mammalian digestive system produces chemicals or enzymes that can break them down. However, plant-eating mammals such as horses are able to make use of these compounds because of the bacteria that live in their intestines (without these bacteria, structural carbohydrates would be about as nutritious as the pages of this book; there's much more on intestinal bacteria in chapter 2). About 50 percent of the major structural carbohydrates of plants can be digested by the horse; what's left passes out in the manure.

Nonstructural carbohydrates are made up of sugars (sweet tasting carbohydrates). There are many types of sugars. They can be simple compounds like glucose (the sugar found in blood) and fructose (found in fruits and honey). Two sugars can be chemically tied together (the resulting compound is called a disaccharide; the *di-* part of the word means "two" and the *-saccharide* refers to the chemical structure of the carbohydrate). Sucrose (found in sugar beets and molasses) and lactose (found in milk) are two disaccharides. If you string a whole bunch of sugars together, you get a compound called a polysaccharide (the prefix *poly-* means "many"). The most important polysaccharide in the horse's diet is starch. Various grains are made up largely of starches.

Even though all starches are made up of a bunch of glucose molecules chemically tied together, the way that the molecules are tied together is different for different grains. This difference in construction directly affects how well a particular starch will be digested by the horse. Of the grains fed to horses, oats have the most easily digestible form of starch, followed by sorghum, corn and barley.

Depending on the diet your horse eats, nonstructural carbohydrates may make up a significant percentage of the energy in its feed. Grass hays contain only a small amount of nonstructural carbohydrates while grain diets are rich in them (but much lower in plant fiber). Pasture (fresh grass) falls somewhere in between.

3

· FIGURE I ·

Fats

Fat is a terrific source of energy for the horse. As anyone who can't get enough ice cream knows, fat provides a lot of calories in a fairly small package. In fact, when you compare equal weights, the digestion of fat provides approximately three times as much energy as oats and two and one-half times as much energy as corn. The most common sources of fat available in the horse's diet are vegetable oils such as corn or soybean oil, animal fat and high-fat stabilized rice bran.

Studies have been done to determine which fats horses like to eat the most. Corn oil has always come out on top, followed by various plant oils like soybean and canola, with animal fat on the bottom. Most horses will turn up their noses at any other type of fat if there is corn oil around. Still, animal fat is a fairly cheap and commonly used source of fat in horses' diets.

Protein

Although it's an important dietary component in its own right (a discussion of protein follows), protein can also be used as a source of energy by the horse. In fact, if you feed protein to a horse beyond that which is required to fulfill his dietary needs, energy is exactly what protein is used for. The problem, from several different metabolic points of view, is that it's not a very *good* source of energy. On a level more dear to your pocketbook, protein is expensive. Actually, it's the most expensive ingredient you can add to a horse's diet. Giving extra protein to a horse is a waste of money.

PROTEIN

Protein is a term used to describe any one of a group of compounds that make up the major part of every cell in the horse's body. There's protein in hair, hoof, skin, muscle and blood cells. Proteins make up the major part of the hormones and enzymes used to control the horse's biologic processes. Protein is used to build new tissues and repair old ones. If you took all the water and fat out of a horse, about 80 percent of what would be left would be protein.

Proteins are made up of smaller building blocks called amino acids. These individual amino acids are chemically hooked together in different orders to make up the many different proteins of the horse's body. Think of the individual amino acids as letters in the alphabet; the finished proteins are the words created by those letters. There are twenty-two different amino acids that are used to make protein.

Amino acids are divided into two groups. *Essential* amino acids are those that must be supplied by the horse's diet or manufactured by the bacteria in the digestive system. *Nonessential* amino acids are those that can be produced in the body tissues (and don't need to be supplied or produced). Although this distinction is very important when considering how to feed people, chickens or pigs, the digestive system of the horse is able to obtain all the amino acids it needs from the bacteria in the digestive system. Thus, mature horses that get enough protein in their diets simply don't have amino acid (or protein) deficiencies.

Unlike carbohydrates and fats, protein contains the element nitrogen (on average, protein is about 16 percent nitrogen). Nitrogen in feed can be easily measured; assuming that every protein has the magic 16 percent nitrogen number in it, the "crude protein" measurement of the feed can be calculated. That figure is then printed on every bag of horse feed that you'll see (it's required!).

When horse owners think about protein and their horse, most of the time they are concerned about the "proper" amount of protein in the horse's feed. Actually, the amount of protein required in a horse's diet depends on such things as the individual horse's protein requirement, the quality of protein being fed (some protein sources are better than others) and the amount of feed the horse is eating. However, given that you may be concerned, the following protein levels are good starting points for the diets of individual horses:

- Mature horses for maintenance: 8–10 percent.
- Mature horses in training: 10–12 percent. (Contrary to what's commonly believed, performance horses do not need high-protein diets. High performance does not equal high protein.)
- Pregnant mares: 11–12 percent.
- Lactating mares: 13–14 percent. (They need the extra protein to help produce milk.)
- Weanling horses: 14.5–16 percent. (This higher level of protein required in the diet of the weanling horse reflects the fact that weanlings need more protein to build body tissues and grow, as well as the fact that they don't eat as much as bigger horses and thus need a more concentrated protein source.)
- Yearling horses: 13–14 percent.

Contrary to what you may have heard, feeding protein in excess of what is needed by the horse isn't really harmful to its health. However, it does have some drawbacks. First, as previously mentioned, feeding excess protein is a waste of money. Second, the horse has to get rid of the nitrogen that's in protein. That's done via the kidneys. Thus, horses on high-protein diets (such as alfalfa hay) may be observed to urinate more (and make a mess of their stalls). Last, the horse has to drink more water to help get rid of the nitrogen; this increased water intake may influence performance by increasing the amount of weight the horse has to carry around (one gallon of water weighs over eight pounds).

VITAMINS

The term *vitamin* is a general one that refers to a number of unrelated compounds occurring in most foods in small amounts. Vitamins are needed for all the normal metabolic functions of the horse's body. Of course, all feed contains various amounts of different vitamins and the diet is an important source of them.

Horse people seem to get pretty worked up about vitamin levels in their horse's diet. Much of this concern is unwarranted. That's because—unlike people—with the exception of vitamins A and E, the horse is able to provide all of its own vitamins. The horse gets those vitamins by production in its own body, from its diet and from absorption of vitamins that are produced in the intestinal tract by bacteria. Theoretically, if horses are provided with plenty of green, good quality forage, the vitamin needs will take care of themselves.

Vitamins are divided into two classes: fat-soluble and water-soluble. While this is mostly a matter of importance to chemists (the classification describes the ability of the vitamins to be dissolved in either fat or water), vitamin solubility does have one more practical implication. Vitamins that are fat-soluble (A, D, E and K) are easily stored in the fat reserves of the horse's body. Water-soluble vitamins like the B vitamins and vitamin C can't be stored for long periods of time since there's no place to keep them. Thus, even though vitamins are important and necessary, they aren't harmless; because of their storage in the horse's body, it's possible to over-supplement fat-soluble vitamins and wind up with *toxicity* (poisoning) problems (especially vitamins A and D; vitamin E isn't stored by the horse's body very well, so there really aren't any toxicity problems with it).

As you undoubtedly know, vitamins are also divided into letter groups. The basic functions of these groups are described here:

8

1. *Vitamin A*   Vitamin A helps to maintain the normal structure and function of the body's *epithelial* cells, the cells that occur on the surface of the body like the skin, the eyes and the lining of the digestive tract. It's also needed for normal bone growth, for maintenance of normal vision and for normal immune system and reproductive functions.

2. *B Vitamins*   The B vitamins are a whole group of vitamins that are responsible for helping with many of the normal metabolic and energy-producing functions of the horse. B vitamins are produced in large amounts by the bacteria of the horse's large intestine; thus, it's pretty much impossible for a healthy horse to become deficient in them. B vitamins are further subdivided into smaller groups and given numbers. Here are those subgroups:

    a. *Vitamin B$_1$ (Thiamine)*   Thiamine is important in the production of energy by the body's cells.

    b. *Vitamin B$_2$ (Riboflavin)*   Riboflavin is important for many normal metabolic activities in the horse and in the production of energy. It's a bit difficult to figure out *exactly* what riboflavin does since it's not possible to make a diet for horses that's deficient in it.

    c. *Vitamin B$_3$ (Pantothenic Acid)*   Pantothenic acid helps in the production of energy by the horse's cells.

    d. *Vitamin B$_6$*   Actually, there are three different compounds that go under the name of B$_6$. Among other things, this group of vitamins helps to break down amino acids, the building blocks from which proteins are made, so they can be used by the horse's body.

    e. *Vitamin B$_{12}$ (Cynaocobolamin)* Vitamin B$_{12}$ is needed by the horse's body so that the oxygen-carrying red blood cells can mature.

    f. *Folic acid*   A B vitamin without a number, folic acid is important in the production of red blood cells, as well as in the synthesis of DNA (the compound that has all the genetic information of the horse).

    g. *Niacin*   Another numberless B vitamin, niacin is involved in generating energy for the horse.

    h. *Biotin*   Sometimes called Vitamin H, biotin is needed for the normal growth of hoof and hair.

3. *Vitamin C*   Also known as ascorbic acid, Vitamin C is essential for the health of various epithelial surfaces and membranes. It's not possible to make a diet for horses that's deficient in vitamin C, especially since, unlike humans, horses synthesize their own vitamin C in their bodies.

4. *Vitamin D*   Vitamin D is needed for the normal growth and development of bones. It's produced in the horse's body when the horse is exposed to sunlight (hence the term "sunshine vitamin"), and it's stored in the liver. Consequently, it's not very easy to make horses deficient in vitamin D unless you never let them outside and keep them covered up.

5. *Vitamin E*   Vitamin E is needed in the horse's diet for reproduction, normal muscle development, the normal function of red blood cells, the immune and nervous systems and many other biochemical functions. It's found in fairly high levels in various grains and especially in green forages.

6. *Vitamin K*   The K group of vitamins promotes clotting of the blood. Deficiencies of Vitamin K are not known to exist in horses.

To ensure an adequate supply of vitamins for your horse, make sure that you feed good quality, fresh feed (this recommendation is repeated often in this book; see chapter 4 for lots of information on feed). Once hay is cut, dried and put into storage, the vitamin content begins to decrease as it reacts with the oxygen in the air (this process, called oxidation, is the same one that causes metal to rust). If it's hot and humid where the hay is stored, the rate of decrease in the vitamin content of hay speeds up. Depending on how the hay is put up and kept, its vitamin content can virtually disappear within three months. Decreasing vitamin content can also be a problem with grain concentrates and vitamin supplements, but most vitamin suppliers coat their vitamins with gelatin to help prevent oxidation.

MINERALS (ASH)

Minerals are *inorganic* (that is, they don't contain the element carbon) substances that are needed by the horse for normal metabolic and biologic activity. Unlike vitamins, minerals cannot be formed by the horse; thus they have to come into the horse's body from dietary sources. Fortunately, most feeds given to the horse contain a variety of important minerals.

The mineral content of various feedstuffs varies depending on the soils in which the feed is grown. Thus, it's a common practice to provide horses with trace mineral and salt blocks "just in case." This practice is certainly harmless, (although if your horse decides to pass the time by eating his salt block, it can get a bit expensive). That's not to say that the products are particularly useful; performance horses, pregnant and lactating mares and growing horses cannot get enough minerals in their diet from trace mineral salt (when you actually look at these products, you will find that they are mostly just salt). Minerals are also provided in processed grain products that have been fortified by adding vitamin and mineral premixes (see chapter 4) and in a virtually endless number of supplements that are available to feed the horse (see chapter 5). Even though minerals are needed by the horse, *they should only be supplemented to correct for specific mineral deficiencies in the horse's diet. Too much mineral supplementation is as bad or worse than too little.* Minerals are often divided into two broad categories based on the amounts needed in the diet.

Macrominerals ("Major" Minerals)

As the name implies, *macrominerals* are those that are needed in the diet in larger amounts than their "micro" cousins. Important macrominerals for which functions are known in the horse include:

1. *Calcium*   Calcium's most important function is as a structural component for bone. It's also required for normal muscle function in the horse. The control of calcium metabolism is very complex and associated with vitamin D; apparently the horse does a pretty good job of regulating calcium levels since problems pertaining to dietary calcium are virtually unheard of in the horse if it is properly fed.

2. *Phosphorus*   Phosphorus is required for normal development of the skeleton as well as for numerous metabolic functions. The levels of phosphorus are closely associated with calcium levels in the horse. The "balance" between calcium and phosphorus in the diet (called the calcium:phosphorus ratio) has been closely studied in the horse. Balances of anywhere from 1.1:1 to 6:1 (calcium:phosphorus) have been reported in both growing and adult horses with no adverse effects on the horses. It appears that the balance between the two minerals is less important than making sure that the absolute dietary requirements are met.

3. *Magnesium*   Magnesium is required for many of the enzyme functions needed for the production of energy. It's found in the fluid that exists both within and outside the cells of the horse's body.

4. *Sulfur* Sulfur is a structural component found in highest levels in hoof and hair.

Electrolytes

Electrolytes are macrominerals that, when dissolved in water, are capable of conducting electricity. There is electrical activity going on constantly in the horse's body, especially in relation to the normal function of the horse's muscles and nerves, and the dissolved electrolytes allow this activity to happen. Table salt (sodium chloride) is one type of electrolyte; others include potassium and calcium.

Microminerals (Trace Minerals)

Microminerals are required in very small amounts by the horse's body (hence the term *trace* mineral). They can be shown to occur in the diet: but the horse doesn't need very much of them, and their purpose in the horse's body often isn't known. They exist in interrelationships that are very complex and poorly understood. In fact, some trace minerals (for example, aluminum) can be shown to exist in normal tissue but have no known functions. Although they are of biologic importance to horses, as a practical matter, most trace minerals are required in only small amounts by the horse. With a couple of important exceptions (see chapter 5), signs of specific trace mineral deficiencies or toxicities are rarely reported in the horse.

That said, there are a few important trace minerals for which the function is known. These minerals should be considered when you are putting together a diet for your horse:

1. *Copper* Copper is involved in blood and bone production and normal skin pigmentation. It's also required for the normal function of many of the enzyme systems of the horse's body. Copper

is required for the normal absorption of iron; relationships also exist between it and the trace minerals molybdenum and zinc. Problems caused by too much copper in the diet are pretty much unknown in the horse.

2. *Iron*   Iron is needed for the transport of oxygen by the red blood cells of the horse's body. Neither iron deficiencies nor toxicities are reported in the horse, but too much iron in the diet can interfere with the absorption of other minerals.

3. *Zinc*   Zinc is important in many enzyme systems associated with the development of the horse's skeleton and with the normal functioning of the horse's immune system. The zinc intake of horses on diets made up solely of forage may be marginal.

4. *Selenium*   Selenium is needed for normal muscle and immune functions.

5. *Manganese*   The best known function of manganese is its role in the formation of bone and cartilage.

6. *Iodine*   The only known function of iodine is as part of the hormones produced by the horse's thyroid gland (these are important hormones in the control of the horse's metabolism).

You can go a little nutty worrying too much about trace minerals in your horse's diet. The last thing in the world that is going to hold back your horse is a deficiency in something like fluorine or molybdenum. As a practical matter, if the amounts of selenium, copper and zinc are normal in your horse's diet, levels of most other trace minerals will be, too. If you do want to add trace minerals to your horse's diet, do so with care. You can ask you veterinarian, an agriculture extension agent or animal nutritionist (local universities are frequently a good source of nutritionists) about specific mineral deficiencies that occur in your particular area.

Chelated Minerals

A number of minerals, such as zinc, iron or magnesium, are metallic substances. *To chelate* means "to bind a metal element to another substance." In the case of minerals, they are often bound to amino acids, the building blocks from which protein is made.

Manufacturers claim that chelated minerals are absorbed more quickly and efficiently by the horse's body than their nonchelated brethren. Depending on the species that's studied, this may or may not be true. Research in people has shown that chelated minerals are rapidly separated from the amino acids they are bound to in the stomach and intestines; they are then absorbed just like nonchelated minerals. In cattle, chelation appears to offer the minerals some protection from the bacteria that occur in the first part of the bovine digestive tract. However, there's no evidence to date that chelation of minerals offers the horse any nutritional advantage.

WATER

For all the talk about all the things you feed your horse, water is the single most important thing in its diet. A horse can lose almost all of its body fat and over 50 percent of its body protein and still be healthy (though skinny). However, a loss of only 10 percent of the body's water is devastating. Water functions as a coolant and as a universal solvent for many of the chemical reactions in the horse's body and is critical to maintain blood pressure.

The actual water requirement of the horse can vary greatly depending on such things as environmental temperature, exercise activity, lactation and the type of feed consumed. Although the precise amounts of water required for various activities have been studied, as a practical matter, you should always make sure that your horse has unlimited access to fresh, clean water (that makes things much easier on both of you). As a rule, the sources of water for the horse, from the most to the least desirable, are spring water, fresh city water, well water, running creeks or rivers and, finally, lakes and small stock ponds. Optimum water consumption occurs when the water is between 45 and 75 degrees Fahrenheit (7 and 24 degrees Celsius). Thus, such things as water heaters, while unquestionably a convenience for the horse owner (there's nothing worse than having to get up early in the morning to break up the ice in your horse's water trough), are also a good way to help ensure that horses drink adequate quantities of water when the weather is cold.

Common sense is an invaluable commodity when it comes to supplying water for your horse. Although it's not much fun, water buckets and tanks should be routinely cleaned. Automatic and/or heated waterers should be checked regularly to make sure that they are in good working order (such things as a small electric current running though a heated water supply will make a horse understandably reluctant to drink). Since water is so very important for your horse's health, if there's any question about the quality of the water that your horse is getting, it's not a bad idea to get it analyzed.

Water can occasionally be the source of trouble for the horse. Too much water is not really a problem, although horses that drink lots of water to pass the time in their stalls can be a bit of a nuisance because of the urine puddles they so liberally create. On the other hand, reduced water consumption is associated with some types of colic (see chapters 10 and 11 for more information on nutrition and colic). Dehydration can be a serious problems in horses that exercise heavily (such as endurance horses); for that reason, water drinking should be encouraged at all times while horses are exercising (although when a horse stops exercising, he should be watered in small amounts as he cools out to prevent problems related to water overload).

Believe it or not, that's pretty much all there is to any kind of feed that you can give your horse. All you have to worry about is supplying your horse with sufficient quantities of five things: energy, protein, vitamins, minerals and water. The next step in your mission of making the feeding of your horse understandable and easy is to figure out how the horse uses the stuff that makes up his feed. That's the subject of the next chapter.

CHAPTER 2

The Horse's Digestive System

Different animals appear to have tried different approaches to solving life's problems. Some work; some don't. Take the problem of how to get around quickly (if you're being chased, for example). Which way do you get around: on two or four legs? Clearly, most land-dwelling mammals successfully solved this question by staying on all fours. Using all four legs, animals can move much more quickly than those that ended up using only two. Thus, one could argue that at least insofar as getting around quickly goes, four legs is a better solution to the problem than two because more animals use four legs than two. (Those that decided to use two ultimately did okay but had to find other ways to adapt, such as living in trees or driving cars; it ends up that using the other two limbs for things other than running around offers some advantages, too).

Different approaches to solving the problem of how to get nutrition from the food that's taken into the body have been tried by mammals, too. All mammals have apparently figured out that before you can do anything with food, it has to be reduced to a smaller size. It's much easier for the body to process small pieces of food than large ones. Thus, all mammals chew and grind their food to some degree. But in addition to chewing, mammals have come up with two other approaches to breaking food down into its component parts so it can be used by the body.

The first approach is to break down the food, using various chemicals and enzymes. *Enzymes* are proteins that help speed up various chemical reactions that occur throughout the horse's body. (In the horse, they are particularly important in helping to break down the plant materials that horses eat.) Chemicals such as hydrochloric acid (which is produced in the horse's stomach) also help to break apart food that's taken in by the horse. After food is reduced to its component parts by enzymatic or chemical digestion, the various parts are then absorbed into the blood stream and employed by the body to maintain life.

The second approach to breaking down food involves the process of fermentation (the same process that's used to make beer and other alcoholic beverages). Fermentation employs specialized bacteria that live in the mammal's body. The process of fermentation decomposes foodstuffs into particular products that can yield energy; a by-product of the process is gas.

Most mammals use both the chemical/enzyme and fermentation approaches to digestion. The most successful approach to digestion (at least if you judge by the number of animals that employ it) is used by cows, goats, giraffes, gnus and other ruminants. After briefly chewing it, ruminants put their food into a large fermentation vat called the *rumen*. There, the ingested food is broken down by bacteria. After the chewed food sits in the rumen for a bit, it's regurgitated back up into the mouth (the cud that a cow chews is this bit of fermented feed), chewed again and swallowed. The feed then goes through a chemical and enzyme process where more nutrients are extracted. What's left unused (mostly indigestible plant fiber) comes out the back end of the intestinal tract.

Some mammals use primarily the chemical and enzyme route to digestion. These are simple-stomached creatures like dogs, cats, pigs and people. Simple-stomached animals begin to break down their feed in the stomach, continuing the process throughout the upper portion of the small intestines, removing nutrients and water along the way and eliminating what's not used.

How Horses Digest Their Feed

Horses represent a very small group of mammals that put their food through the chemical/enzyme process *before* fermenting it. This group of contrarian digesters is pretty much limited to the horse, the rabbit, the elephant and the rhinoceros. The biggest problem with reversing the ruminant process is that the gas that's produced as a by-product of fermentation doesn't have an easy way out. Cows tend to burp a lot because the rumen is pretty close to the mouth; there's no close, convenient outlet for the gas produced by the horse's digestive tract (but you can often hear it when it escapes).

Like every other mammal, horses begin the digestive process by taking their feed into the mouth and chewing it, using a combination of their sensitive, mobile lips and the front teeth (called the incisors) to pick up the food and their big cheek teeth (the premolars and molars) to grind it up. Of course, for this process to work efficiently, it requires a sound, functional mouth; as part of the care of your horse, you should have its mouth examined regularly by your veterinarian and the teeth *floated* as needed (usually, that's no more than once a year; the term "floating" refers to the teeth being made smooth and level, in the same way that cement is floated when it's poured).

Chewing and the presence of food in the mouth stimulate the flow of saliva. The main purpose of the saliva is to lubricate the feed so that it can pass easily down into the stomach. (Contrary to what you may have heard, saliva doesn't have much other digestive function in the horse). Apparently horses need a lot of lubrication to swallow their feed; research has estimated the saliva production in adult horses at ten to twelve liters per day (that's close to four gallons.)

The swallowed food travels to the horse's stomach via a muscular tube called the esophagus. The stomach of the adult horse is actually rather small, considering the size of the horse; that's also a likely reason that horses in the wild eat most of the time (for seventeen of the twenty-four hours in a day, and as many as twenty-three hours of every day!). The stomach is the starting point for the digestion of the horse's feed, which is accomplished mostly by the action of the acids and enzymes found there. It's also a reservoir for the controlled release of stomach contents into the next part of the digestive tract, the small intestine.

The small intestine is the longest part of the digestive tract of the horse; it's almost seventy feet long and divided into three sections (the duodenum, the jejunum and the ileum). The small intestine (some people also call it the *foregut*) receives an almost continual flow of stomach contents. It also receives "juices" from the pancreas and bile from the liver. The fluids from the pancreas and the liver are rich in digestive enzymes that help break down the feed material in the intestine so it can be absorbed by the horse's body. The small intestine is a busy place; it's the primary site of digestion and absorption of:

- Simple sugars and starches from the digestion of carbohydrates
- Amino acids from the digestion of protein
- Free fatty acids from the digestion of fats
- Fat-soluble vitamins A, D and E
- Some minerals

Anything that can't be digested in the stomach and the small intestine passes on back into the cecum and large colon (known as the *hindgut*). It's in these structures that the process of fermentation occurs. Billions and billions of bacteria and protozoa (little one-celled organisms) go to work in the hindgut to break down the complex molecules that make up feed, especially plant fiber. The intestinal microorganisms produce energy-yielding compounds called *volatile fatty acids* as well as such things as amino acids (the building blocks of protein) and B vitamins. In addition, the hindgut is responsible for the absorption of water and electrolytes (sodium, potassium, chloride and phosphate) from the diet.

Whatever is left passes into the rectum. Undigested fecal material sits in the rectum until enough of it accumulates to stimulate defecation through the anus. The whole process from mouth to anus usually takes from 24 to 72 hours in the horse.

How Feed Affects Your Horse

Although all feeds contain the same things, not all of those things affect horses in the same way. Feeding a horse has some rather profound consequences on its body. If you can understand how your horse uses the components of its feed, you can then supply those components in amounts suitable to help it try to meet whatever goal you have for it.

Everyone who has ever fed a horse has seen how excited horses get when they anticipate that they are going to be fed. There is a measurable response of the horse's cardiovascular system to feeding that actually changes the distribution of blood flow in the horse's body. When fed, the amount of blood that goes to the horse's GI tract increases by as much as 7 percent.

Feeding also increases the amount of weight that's inside the horse. It does so by more than you probably think. It's been estimated that for every 1 kilogram of dry feed that your horse eats (2.2 pounds), the horse ingests about 10 kg of water (this includes salivary water, which is constantly being recycled). Thus, the more fiber a horse eats, the more water is bound in the digestive system and the more weight is carried by the horse.

Once the feed gets inside the horse, it is broken down into its component parts (more on this follows). Once those parts get into the horse's bloodstream, they have to get into the cells. They do this largely through the effects of a hormone called *insulin*. Insulin is sort of a metabolic traffic officer. It directs the flow of nutrients to the various tissues of the horse's body as needed. There are specific receptors for insulin in the tissues; once the insulin binds to those receptors, *glucose* (the end product of the digestion of things used for energy) and *amino acids* (the end product of the digestion of protein) can enter the cells and go to work.

Insulin is produced when the sugar in the blood goes up. This happens after just about anything is fed to your horse. Without insulin, the blood sugar would just go up and up (and you would have a diabetic horse, which, by the way, is not known to exist). Via the action of insulin, the blood sugar is able to enter the tissues, where it is used for the production of energy by the cells. The by-products of energy production are water (which is eliminated in the urine, sweat and the respiratory tract) and carbon dioxide (which exits via the lungs).

Providing energy is the most important consideration in any horse's diet. How the horse uses that energy is critical to an understanding of how to feed your horse, particularly in regards to feeding a performance horse (the subject of chapter 8).

HOW HORSES USE COMPONENTS OF FEED

What Happens to Carbohydrates?

The structural carbohydrates (fiber) which give plants their rigidity are digested in the horse's large intestine (hindgut). The bacteria that live there can break them down into volatile fatty acids, which are then used for energy production. It's a bit of an involved process.

On the other hand, nonstructural carbohydrate digestion is really pretty simple. These carbohydrates are always broken down into the simple sugars (glucose and fructose). The simple sugars are then absorbed directly through the small intestine and into the horse's blood stream (that's why you can get an idea of how well the intestine is working by measuring the glucose in the blood). Disaccharides like the sucrose in molasses or the lactose in milk have to be broken in two before they can be absorbed (this is kid's stuff for the small intestine). All in all, nonstructural carbohydrate digestion is really pretty uncomplicated: except for starch.

Starch, the complex, nonstructural carbohydrate that's a big feature of any sort of grain you feed to your horse, poses a particular problem for the horse's digestive system. Starch isn't digested any differently from any other nonstructural carbohydrate; it's broken down into little pieces and absorbed. However, because it is such a large, complex molecule, if it is fed in large amounts, there may not be enough time for the starch to be completely digested in the horse's small intestine. Nondigested starch continues right down the digestive tract into the large intestine to get digested by the bacteria that live there. This is not a particularly good thing.

The bacteria that digest starch normally make up only a small portion of the bacteria that are living in the large intestine. However, when they are presented with a lot of undigested starch, this bacterial minority undergoes something of a population explosion. While this may be a good thing for getting rid of the starch, it's not necessarily great for the horse's intestine. When starch is digested in the hindgut, one of the end products is lactic acid. Lactic acid irritates the lining of the gut and makes the contents of the bowel more acidic. A more acidic bowel means that the living conditions for the bacteria that digest forage becomes less ideal; as a result, some of those bacteria die and the normal bacterial environment of the hindgut changes.

Many horses seem to do fine being fed large amounts of starch. However, two big horse health problems have been associated with feeding large amounts of grain concentrates (which mean lots of starch) to horses. *Laminitis* (inflammation of the connections between the dead hoof and the sensitive tissue underneath the hoof), can be experimentally produced by feeding an overdose of carbohydrates to the horse (your horse can do the same thing to himself if he breaks into the grain bin). *Colic* (which refers to pain coming from the horse's abdomen), is also seen in greater frequency in horses that eat grain concentrates. The precise reasons why high amounts of starch can cause these problems for horses isn't known. These potentially important complications of feeding large amounts of starch to your horse must be considered when you go to figure out its diet.

Energy that's not immediately used by the horse is stored and used later (say, when a horse has to jump over some fences). One way to store energy is as a chain of sugar called *glycogen*; there are significant glycogen warehouses in muscle tissue (where it's available for immediate service) and in the liver. The other way to store energy is in deposits of fat, which is found just about everywhere in the horse's body (depending on just how fat the horse is).

What Happens to the Protein?

When protein is taken into the horse's body, the "word" of the protein is broken up into amino acid "letters" by the enzymes of the stomach, pancreas and small intestine. Each amino acid is then carried into the blood stream by a process that requires energy. The amino acids are taken in the blood to the cells of the body to be formed into new proteins.

If there are more amino acids provided in the diet than what's needed (that is, too much protein), they travel to the horse's liver, where they are used for the production of energy. Before they can be used for energy, the nitrogen molecule that characterizes proteins has to be broken off. The nitrogen is carried to the kidneys and eliminated in the urine as ammonia. That's why stalls that aren't well ventilated smell so acrid. That's also why the urine of horses that eat only alfalfa hay can smell funny. Furthermore, if a horse eats a lot of protein, it has to produce a lot of urine; that's one reason owners of horses that eat alfalfa hay may complain about their horses soaking their stalls.

What Happens to Fat?

The digestion and absorption of fat by the horse's body is pretty complicated (and mostly of interest to nutritionists). Like almost everything else, fat digestion occurs in the small intestine of the horse (the small intestine is a busy place). Fat is such a big molecule, from a chemical point of view, that it takes the body a bit of time to break it down into usable parts.

Fats are largely made up of components called *fatty acids*. It is the fatty acids that are actually broken down to provide energy for the horse. One source of fatty acids is those that are eaten by the horse. Another source, called *volatile* fatty acids, come from the bacterial digestion that occurs in the hindgut. The fatty acids that are absorbed by the horse eventually end up in the horse's liver, which decides whether the fatty acids will be used by the cells of the body to produce energy or whether they should be stored in little (and sometimes not so little) fat deposits that occur all over the horse's body. The stored fat is a readily available source of energy. Of course, fat stores are not only created by eating too much fat; eating too much energy, from whatever the calorie source, will get your horse fat.

27

What Happens to Vitamins and Minerals?

There are a bunch of different vitamins and minerals; accordingly, there are a bunch of different ways that vitamins and minerals are absorbed and utilized by the horse's body. Once absorbed through the intestinal tract, vitamins and minerals go to work.

Minerals are taken by various transport systems to the individual tissues of the horse's body, where they are used in such things as maintaining the structural framework of the skeleton (calcium and phosphorus) or as a component of systems that regulate the horse's metabolism (such as iodine and the thyroid gland). Minerals are found throughout the horse's body and are lost in feces, urine and sweat. It is certainly possible to have excessive mineral levels in the horse's diet due either to plant toxicities (such as occur with selenium) or overzealous supplementation. Thus, while it's a good idea to ensure that your horse's mineral intake is adequate, more is not necessarily better.

Natural sources of fat-soluble vitamins like A, D, E and K are associated with dietary fat. Thus, when fat is being digested, fat-soluble vitamins are being absorbed, too. Fat-soluble vitamins are stored in the various fat deposits found throughout the horse's body and are excreted by the horse's liver via the bile. On the other hand, water-soluble vitamins aren't stored in any appreciable amounts in the horse's body; they're continually produced by the bacteria in the horse's hindgut. They are turned over rapidly in the horse's body and excreted in the urine. In fact, it's pretty much impossible to make a horse's diet deficient in water-soluble vitamins. Consequently, most nutritionists pay close attention to fat-soluble vitamin levels in feed and pretty much ignore the water-soluble ones. (You should, too.)

What Happens to Water?

Water utilization by the horse's body couldn't be much simpler. It doesn't require any energy for the horse to use water (other than the energy used to swallow). Water simply passes through the intestine into the bloodstream. Water is used as needed for such things as lubrication of feed and cooling of the body; excess water is simply eliminated in the urine and feces.

How Horses Eat

In the wild, horses graze almost all the time. (Where do you think they got the phrase, "eating like a horse"?) Thus, it shouldn't be any sort of surprise that the horse's digestive tract is especially adapted to process and use diets made up of plant material. What people seem to forget is that not only *can* horses digest plant material like hay or pasture, they *must*.

Forage (the term refers to any type of plant material) should be the main ingredient in any horse's diet. It helps horses feel full and provides "chewing satisfaction." A constant source of fiber is essential for the health of the bacteria in the hindgut. Plus, a certain amount of bulk in the horse's diet is needed to sustain normal digestive function.

How often does a horse need to be fed? If you were to try to mimic the "natural" situation, you'd have to feed the horse almost continually. Of course, while continuous feeding might be more natural, it would have some obvious negative implications on your sleep habits. Plus, horses that are in intense athletic training *can't* be fed continuously; horses that are kept in a stall probably *shouldn't* be fed continuously, or they'll get fat.

Studies have shown that once you start feeding more than three times a day, there's no benefit to the horse. Feeding forage as many as sixteen times a day (can you imagine?) offers no dietary advantage over feeding three times a day. If you are going to feed lots of starch (grain) to your horse, it will be beneficial to its digestive tract if you split the grain into several meals. In fact, due to the potential problems with excess starch reaching the hindgut, *you should never feed your horse more than five pounds of grain at any one meal.* Thus, if you want to give your horse fifteen pounds of grain concentrate, do it in at least three separate meals to help avoid any problems.

Now you know what feed contains and how the horse goes about using it. The next step in figuring out how to feed your horse is to know what sorts of feed are available. That's the subject of the next chapter.

CHAPTER 3

Feedstuffs

PASTURE IS THE MOST "NATURAL" WAY TO FEED HORSES. Good quality pasture can be a complete nutritional diet for horses. Plus, it's the cheapest way to feed them.

Good quality pasture should be tasty (for the horse) and nutritious and provide grazing for as much of the year as possible. A mix of grass and clover is one example of such a pasture (research has shown that horses actually prefer a mix of pasture forages). Pasture should be as free of weeds as possible. It should be big enough for the number of horses that are grazing on it to prevent over-grazing and damage to the pasture. A rule of thumb is that there should be two acres of pasture per mature horse if you intend the pasture to be your horse's sole source of energy. (Horse hooves are harder on the ground than are the hooves of other animals that eat pasture.) If pastures are managed intensively, they may be able to support more grazing. However, the ability of an individual horse to maintain its body weight on pasture alone depends also on individual factors such as the horse's age and temperament. Of course, the pasture should be free of poisonous plants and free of junk such as old cars, wire, stumps and big rocks. It should be enclosed with a safe fence; if you use barbed wire around your horse pasture, be prepared for big veterinary bills.

Wet, low-lying areas are normally not good pastures. Such areas drain poorly and breed insects and disease-causing bacteria. Plus, certain types of plants won't grow well in wet areas. Neither should pastures be located on steep slopes. Although horses can move up and down the slopes, steep terrain usually can't support dense plant growth. As a result, such areas frequently become heavily eroded and rutted if they are grazed.

Horses graze selectively. They will eat some areas of a pasture until it's mowed down to nothing (these areas are called *lawns*) while they'll let other areas grow until the plants become so mature that they lose much of their nutritional value (these areas are called *roughs*). You shouldn't count these undesirable areas when you try to figure out how many horses your pasture can support. If the pasture is too uneven with lawns and roughs, it should be clipped.

Horses tend to defecate in the roughs; normally, horses don't eat where they defecate, but they will eat the roughs if there isn't enough pasture to go around. If there is a lot of manure in the pasture, many people drag it to spread it out. Even though it's a common practice, you have to be careful about dragging manure through a pasture because it can spread parasite eggs. You should normally drag a pasture during the hot summer months only, leaving the pasture open for a few weeks after dragging before returning the horses to it. An even better solution than dragging (so as not to spread parasites) is to remove or vacuum the manure from the pasture.

It's usually better to have several smaller pastures than one big one; this allows horses to graze the smaller pastures more intensely and evenly.

When one pasture is eaten down, you can move the horses to the new pasture and let the old one regrow.

The nutrient content of pasture can vary depending on the time of the year. Spring grass in many areas is lush. The high water content in lush grasses dilutes the nutrients in the plant. In addition, spring pasture is low in structural carbohydrates; even when they're consuming all they can hold, horses on lush spring grass may not get enough dietary fiber. Later in the season, green pasture can fool you in a different way. Horses will eat grass species selectively, picking through the salad bar for just those items they find the tastiest. By midsummer in a dry year, often all that's left are the roughs, which are not in the horses' best nutritional interests.

Fortunately, an easy solution to pasture problems exists; simply offer moderately good grass hay to your horses in pasture. If their fiber and energy needs are being met by the pasture, they will ignore the hay. If the grass is lush and full of water, however, you'll find that the horses will consume the hay, even though there's lots of green stuff for them to eat in the field.

GREEN CHOP

In countries such as New Zealand and Jamaica and in South America, fresh forage can be cut and fed to horses (and other animals) without drying it or storing it in fermentation pits (this process is called *ensiling*). This high-quality feed is known as "green chop."

Green chop is a very good thing to be able to feed to a horse. Horses that live in confinement can still eat as though they were on pasture when fed green chop. Pastures on which the feed is grown don't get abused by the horse; therefore, the available forage can be used to the maximum extent possible. Plus, chopping the forage into little pieces allows grasses to be used as horse feed that might ordinarily not be suitable because of broad leaves and thick stems (things like king or elephant grass).

The problem with green chop is that in order to feed the stuff, you need a very cheap source of labor to cut the forage every day. That, and the fact that it can't be stored, are probably the main reasons why green chop is not fed more frequently to horses.

A variant of green chop found in more manicured surroundings, lawn trimmings, should generally not be fed to horses, especially if you let them sit around (they rapidly begin to ferment). Furthermore, lawn trimmings can contain any number of lovely landscaping plants, some of which are potentially poisonous.

HAYS

A long time ago, somebody figured out that if you cut and dry the plants and grasses that horses eat, they can be stored and fed at a later date. Feeding dried plant material (known as *hay*, which comes from an Old High German word, *hewi*, referring to "that which is mowed") to horses has in large part enabled horses to be domesticated.

Depending on where in the world you live, many different types of hays may be available to feed to horses. Hays have many things in common; they all have essential fiber and varying amounts of energy, protein, vitamins and minerals. However, particular types of hays can be quite different in the nutrients they provide to horses. The nutrient content of particular batches of hay can vary, as well, and this content is affected by the maturity of the hay and the way the hay is processed, among other things.

Hays can be generally divided into two groups. Legume hays are plants that have microorganisms associated with their root systems. These microscopic bugs are able to use the nitrogen that's in the air and soil to produce protein. Hay made from grass plants or cereal grains make up the second group. Compared to legume hays, grass and cereal grain hays typically contain:

- Lower amounts of protein
- Less energy
- Less calcium
- Fewer vitamins
- More digestible fiber

Legumes

Alfalfa hay has been fed to horses longer than any other feed in reported history (since about 500 B.C.). Excellent climatic conditions, including plenty of warm weather and the ability to control the rainfall (by turning the irrigation system on and off) make the western United States alfalfa headquarters. High-quality, western alfalfa hay is in demand for export to horse operations throughout the United States and the world. A significant amount of alfalfa is also produced in the northeast and mid-west regions of the United States. In some parts of the world (such as in Europe, Australia and New Zealand), alfalfa hay is also called *lucerne* hay.

The high protein, energy and calcium content of alfalfa hay make it excellent for young, growing horses and pregnant or lactating mares. Since alfalfa (like other legume hays) is characteristically high in calcium and low in phosphorus, supplemental phosphorus is a good idea if you're feeding your horse a diet made up mainly of alfalfa. Of course, this isn't any different from considerations that you might have to take into account with other hays. Certain hays are higher or lower in one thing or another; depending on the nutrients the hay provides, you may want to add some sort of grain concentrate or supplement to create a balanced diet.

Clover is another legume that's commonly found in pastures. Several varieties of clover exist; Ladino clover is probably the best choice for seeding along with pasture grass to increase the nutrient content of the pasture. Bird's-foot trefoil and lespedeza are two other legumes that can be fed to horses. Both have some advantages over alfalfa in that they can grow in somewhat less favorable environmental conditions, but both are less nutritious and have lower yields than alfalfa. Bird's-foot trefoil and lespedeza are commonly used in seed mixtures for horse pasture.

Grasses

In many parts of the world, horses are maintained mainly on grass plants, many of which can be made into good quality hays. Grass hays are divided into two types, based on the time of year they grow.

Cool season grasses include (but are not limited to):

- *Timothy* Timothy hay is adapted to cool, nonhumid climates but doesn't do well in drought conditions; thus, it is grown primarily in northern and mountain areas of the United States.
- *Orchard grass* Orchard grass is a fast-growing grass that, while able to withstand shady conditions, is very sensitive to overgrazing.
- *Bluegrass* Bluegrass is grown throughout the United States but is most prevalent in the northeastern and north central parts of the country. Bluegrass is very nutritious and forms a dense sod (that's why it's in so many front yards); the dense sod can help withstand the grazing pressure that horses inflict on pastures.
- *Bromegrass* Bromegrass is one of the most drought-tolerant cool-season grasses. It grows well in the corn belt region of the United States.
- *Ryegrass* Ryegrass has the distinction of being the most common grass used in pastures for horses. It has a fine stem and is very nutritious. Unfortunately, ryegrass can occasionally become infected

by a bacteria. Annual ryegrass toxicosis is most commonly reported in sheep and cattle, but a few cased have been reported in horses. Happily, this does not appear to be a common problem.

- *Reed canarygrass* Reed canarygrass is similar to bromegrass in that it can withstand drought conditions, but it also grows well in wet soil. Thus, it can often be found growing in ditches and waterways. Reed canarygrass is not very tasty for horses if it is mature and coarse.

- *Fescue* Fescue is a hardy grass that can tolerate both foot traffic and summer heat. It doesn't seem to be all that tasty for horses until after a frost; then the sugar content goes up and horses seem to like it better. Unfortunately, many varieties of fescue grass are infected with a fungus that can cause all sorts of reproductive problems in brood mares (including failure to produce milk, retained and/or thickened placentas, prolonged gestation and stillbirths) and reduced growth rates in young horses. Newer varieties of fungus-free fescue have been developed that may eventually eliminate the problem of fescue toxicity, but infected fescue is present in many native pastures. It's a reasonably nutritious grass for most horses. If you're con-cerned, the only way to get rid of fescue is to kill the grass, plow it under and start over. The best way to avoid the effects of fescue toxicity is to avoid fescue or to supplement the horses with legume hay.

As their name implies, warm season grasses thrive in the heat and grow well during the warm summer months; they don't do well in areas with cold winter temperatures. These grasses are common to the southern regions of the United States. Unfortunately, it can be hard to make good hay out of some of these grasses because the high humidity and constant rainfall in the areas where they commonly grow keep the cut grass from adequately drying so that it can be baled without fear of mold developing. Warm season grasses that are commonly fed to horses include:

- *Bermuda grass* Bermuda grass adapts well to sandy soil conditions and tolerates grazing animal foot traffic well.
- *Coastal Bermuda grass* Coastal Bermuda grass is one of the highest yielding of the Bermuda grasses. It's used extensively for hay production in the southern United States.
- *Bahia grass* Like Bermuda grass, Bahia grass stands up well to grazing and foot traffic. However, Bahia grass does not respond well in mineral-deficient soils and yields less than does Bermuda grass.
- *Pangola grass* Pangola grass thrives in areas with high heat and high moisture. Unfortunately, those two conditions also preclude the making of high-quality hay from pangola grass.

Grain Hays (Oat, Barley and Wheat)

Cereal grain plants make perfectly good hay as long as the grain hasn't been harvested and the plants are still green (if the grain has been taken and the plants are mature, you get straw). Grain hays are similar to grass-type forages in their nutritional value.

STRAW

Yes, straw. Straw can be made from the stem of any type of grain (wheat, oat, barley, rye) after the seed head has been taken off. In the United States, wheat straw is most commonly used for bedding; other countries find that straw can make good horse feed. In general, straw is higher in fiber and lower in protein and digestible energy than other feeds.

In France, oat straw is quite popular as a feed. It's usually provided in addition to hay and grain. In fact, there is research that shows that it's possible to sustain performance horses on a diet of straw and grain concentrate.

In England and Australia, horses eat a lot of chopped-up straw or poorer quality hay, with or without molasses added to make it taste better. The resultant feed is called *chaff*. There are many variations on basic chaff, but the idea behind feeding it is to give the horse something to eat to keep it occupied without providing too much energy. The U.S. version of chaff is chopped-up alfalfa or grain hay (such as oat) covered with a thick coat of molasses ("A & M" or "O & M").

HAYLAGE AND SILAGE

In some areas of the world, it's hard to make hay because it rains all the time (you know who you are). In these areas, cut forage can be stored in a high-moisture state as haylage or silage. The nutritional content of good silage and haylage (both are fermented plant products) is similar to hay. In the United States, haylage and silage are not typically fed to horses because there are plenty of dry spots in which to grow hay. However, in places such as England and Holland, haylage and silage can be a suitable alternative to dried hays.

GRAINS

Grains are small, dry, one-seeded fruits of cereal plants such as corn, oats and barley. As a rule, grains contain about 50 to 60 percent more energy than an equivalent weight of hay because they are much more efficiently digested by the horse. Just about any grain can be fed to horses, although there are differences between the various grains that need to be considered prior to incorporating any of them into your feed program. Horses are fed grain as a source of extra energy that might be needed for performance, growth, optimum reproduction or lactation (of course, grains contain all of the other stuff that's in any other feed, as well).

Corn (Maize)

More corn is fed to animals than any other feed. Of all the grains, corn provides the highest amount of energy. This means that if you feed your horse corn, you can feed less of it and get the same amount of energy as more of another feed (one quart of corn provides about as much energy as two quarts of oats, for example). This also means that you have to be a bit more careful when feeding corn to your horse, so as not to overfeed. Still, corn offers several advantages over other grains: It costs less, it's of more consistently good quality and it's the only grain with any significant vitamin A activity.

Corn should be processed before it is fed to horses, since the starch in corn is relatively hard for the horse to digest in its small intestine. Corn can be fed in many forms: cracking, flaking or rolling are common methods of processing that improve the digestibility of corn starch. You should probably avoid feeding your horse ground corn because it's so dusty. In South America, many horses eat hominy feed. Hominy is what remains of the corn grain after the corn flour is removed (to be eaten by people).

Oats

Oats seem to be the preferred grain of horsemen. The reasons for this aren't completely clear, but it may indirectly relate to the fact that oats have a higher fiber content than most other grains. With higher fiber, oats are less likely to be overfed than other grains and thus are less likely to cause such things as colic, obesity and laminitis. Oats also tend to be higher in protein than other grains. Furthermore, the starch contained in the grain is more easily digested than are other plant starches, meaning that oat starch is more likely to be digested in the small intestine, where it belongs. Still, it's not that oats are a better feed for horses, it's just that people may be less easily able to mess things up while feeding their horses.

On the down side, oat quality can vary tremendously from plump, starch-filled kernels to those containing mostly fiber. Fiber is much lighter than starch; thus, a coffee can of fibrous oats may weigh much less than one of high-quality oats. You should always feed your horse by the weight of the feed (no matter what feed you choose), not by the volume.

Barley

Barley is a great grain to feed to horses. It falls somewhere between oats and corn in the amount of fiber, energy and protein provided. Barley is commonly included in grain mixes and "sweet feeds" for horses, mostly in the western United States. Like most grains, barley should be processed before it's given to your horse, so that its digestibility is improved.

Grain Sorghum

Grain sorghum is sort of a catch-all term to describe a number of varieties of grain with unusual names like milo, hegari and feterita (among others). Like corn, it's a high-energy, low-fiber grain, so you should be a bit cautious with it. Grain sorghum has a small, hard kernel and must be processed before you feed it to a horse to improve its digestibility. It's a very acceptable feed for horses, although it apparently has a slightly bitter taste that some horses don't like. Grain sorghum (especially milo) is a frequent addition to mixed grain products.

Rye

Rye isn't fed very often to horses; it's used mostly to produce bread and whiskey for human consumption. Most horses don't like the taste of rye, so it's usually mixed with other grains when it's fed. It's very much like barley in its nutritional content and needs to be processed before it's fed to a horse.

You do have to be a little careful feeding rye to horses. Rye may contain a fungus that produces a chemical called ergot. Ergot can cause a decrease in blood flow to the feet, resulting in laminitis; it also causes abortions in pregnant mares.

Wheat

Wheat has about the same nutritional profile as corn, although depending on the type of wheat, it can contain a good amount of protein. It's not fed very often to horses, however, because most wheat goes into making bread for human consumption. Many people feel that if you feed too much wheat to a horse, it will form a doughy ball in the intestinal tract and cause colic (although there's not any published data to support this assertion). Still, if for no other reason, you're most likely not going to be feeding any wheat to your horse because it's expensive compared to other grain products. If you do feed wheat, it should be processed to improve its digestibility.

Even though wheat grain is rarely fed to horses, a lot of byproducts from the processing of wheat for flour are used in making horse feed. *Wheat middlings* and *wheat mill run* are specific terms used to describe these byproducts, which are fairly low in fiber and add some energy and a little bit of protein to whatever they are mixed with. Wheat bran, a frequently fed byproduct of the milling process, is discussed a bit later.

PROTEIN SUPPLEMENTS

To increase the protein content of grain products, many feed manufacturers add supplemental protein. Most of the protein supplements used in horse feed come from plant sources. The plant proteins are usually made from the seed of plants that have had the oil extracted from them. The resultant protein products are up to 50 percent protein and contain a few vitamins and minerals; they are very low in fiber. Common sources of protein in horse feed include:

- *Soybean meal* This is the number one protein supplement used in animal feed in the United States. Soybeans, like alfalfa, are a legume plant.

- *Cottonseed meal* Number two on your animal protein supplement list, is obtained, as you might guess, from the seed of the cotton plant.

- *Linseed meal* This is the product you get when you take the oil out of flax seed. Linseed meal has a reputation for putting a shiny coat on a horse; this may be due to some leftover fat in the meal or merely because people who take the trouble to feed their horse well tend to take care of them, too (and brush them and do other things that help promote a shiny coat).

- *Dehydrated alfalfa meal* This is alfalfa that has been finely ground and heat dried. It is pretty uniform in composition and has to meet certain composition guarantees. It's a good source of protein, minerals and vitamins.

- *Brewer's dried grains* When you allow barley grain to sprout, you get barley malt. Barley malt is used to manufacture a number of alcoholic beverages; the dried, extracted residue of barley malt, along with some dried, spent hops (hops is another grain used in the making of beer) can be fed to horses. The product, which is called brewer's dried grains, is high in fiber and protein.

- *Canola meal* This protein supplement comes from the seed of a European plant called *rape* (it's a member of the mustard family). It's very commonly fed to horses in Canada, if for no other reason than because Canada is one of the world's largest growers of rape seed.

OTHER FEEDS

Beet Pulp

Beet pulp is a byproduct of the process of making table sugar from sugar beets. Chips of the sugar beet are dried after the sugar has been extracted from them and are shredded to make the pulp. Beet pulp is a good source of fiber for horses, and it's also a good source of energy; in fact, it provides about the same amount of energy as do oats. Beet pulp is also a pretty good source of calcium.

It is often recommended that people feed beet pulp after soaking it in water. Tales of dry beet pulp absorbing water and swelling up inside the horse's intestine aren't supported by any clinical reports of such a problem, however. Still, soaking beet pulp prior to feeding it does help keep the dust down (which may be an important consideration if your horse has airway problems). Pelleted forms of beet pulp are also available.

Molasses

Molasses is a syrup that's obtained during the sugar-refining process. It's commonly added to horse feeds to help keep the dust down in feed and to add a sweet taste.

For some reason, many horse owners are concerned about feeding their horse molasses, thinking that it is some sort of a "super energy" food that will turn an otherwise calm horse into a bucking bronco. In fact, molasses has less energy than corn or barley have. In experimental studies, about the only thing that molasses does seem to do is make horses eat faster (they like the taste).

Bran

When the soft, inner kernel of the wheat plant is milled to make flour, a byproduct is the reddish-brown flakes of the outer husk of the grain. In general, there's not much use for the stuff; however, at some time, some enterprising miller found that it could be fed to horses.

Wheat bran is relatively high in digestible fiber, protein and calories. It also has a lopsided calcium-to-phosphorus ratio of about 1 part calcium to 12 parts phosphorus. In the relatively small amounts that bran is normally fed, this isn't that big a deal. If bran is virtually the only thing that a horse gets to eat, however (as was the case in some horses around the turn of the twentieth century), horses develop a disease known as "big head" (so-called because the lack of calcium in the diet causes bone to demineralize; the bone is replaced by soft tissue that gives the horse's skull a lumpy and enlarged look).

Bran has achieved something of an exalted status in the diet of many horses in the prevention and treatment of colic, as a way to make the horse warmer or just as a good healthy treat. It's also been criticized as having no nutritive value and as something that can cause a horse to form enteroliths (intestinal "stones"). There appears to be little truth to any of these ideas; such myths are addressed in detail in the final chapter.

Rice Bran

Rice bran is one of the newer feedstuffs that have come onto the equine market. Like bran that's made from wheat, rice bran is relatively high in fiber, protein and calories. Its calcium-to-phosphorus ratio is also heavily in favor of phosphorus. What makes rice bran so interesting is that a significant portion of its calories come from fat.

Rice bran typically contains about 20 percent fat; that's more fat than just about anything else you can give to a horse, with the exception of animal or vegetable fats. One pound of rice bran contains about the same amount of fat as one-half cup of vegetable oil. The combination of good fiber content and high fat make it a good addition to the diet of some performance horses.

Vegetable Oils

Vegetable oils are a source of energy in the horse's diet. Vegetable oil is just liquid fat. It is extracted from the plant's seeds, using some combination of pressure, heat and chemical solvents. Horses seem to prefer corn oil above all others, but any plant oil can be fed to horses to provide some extra calories (oils don't contain anything else).

By the way, mineral oil, which is commonly used in the treatment of colic in horses, has no caloric value at all. Horses can't digest it.

Miscellaneous Things Fed to Horses Around the World

As you look at what people feed to their horses, it becomes pretty apparent that there's more than one way to do it (as there is with things like cat skinning). It's kind of fun to hear about all the different things horses get to eat around the world. This kind of knowledge will help you keep your neighbor at bay when he or she asserts that there's only one proper way to feed a horse (and that you're doing it all wrong):

- Whole sugarcane (minus the leaves) is ground up and fed to horses in Colombia and other sugar cane producing countries. The leaves can be chopped up into small pieces and fed, too.
- Day-old bread is fed to horses in Spain, mostly as a treat.
- In Holland, when there is a bumper crop of potatoes, horses get to eat some of them. Dutch horses also are fed turnips and the huge winter carrots that are grown there.
- In England, you can buy horse feed flavored (flavoured?) with ground mint leaves.
- In Ireland, horses that were under the care of the famous Thoroughbred trainer Vincent O'Brien received a liter of stout and two eggs in their feed (beer is just water, yeast and fermented grain).
- Although they are primarily a treat in the United States, in England and South Africa, sliced carrots are routinely added to horse

diets because they are thought to help keep horses from going off feed.

- French endurance horses are fed honey during races.
- In India, horses get a treat called *jaggery*, which is big, brown chunks of unrefined cane sugar. *Ghee*, a fat used in cooking, is sometimes added as a source of calories. Indian horses may find their grain ration mixed with cow's milk, too.
- In Abu Dhabi and Dubai, horses may be fed freshly cut lucerne (alfalfa) hay every day.
- In Australia, whole sunflowers may be fed to horses. (The plants are a good source of fat and fiber and have some protein in them, too).
- In some parts of the Middle East, dates without pits are wadded together to make a ball and fed to horses as a treat.
- In some Caribbean countries, the coconut is a food source for horses. Horses can be fed coconut meat or the brown fibers from inside the husk. Coconut meal is an alternative source of protein, and coconut oil is an alternative source of dietary fat.

There are undoubtedly many other things that can be (and are) fed to horses around the world. The point is that horses can be successfully maintained on any number of feeds, since all feeds have the same stuff in them. Feeding a horse is mostly a matter of finding out what feeds are available in your area, learning what the feeds contain and feeding the best quality of those feeds that are available. The next chapter will help you understand what those available feeds are.

CHAPTER 4

Making Horse Feed

Nature intended horses to graze off the grasses and move around the land. Given the advent of things like interstate highways and housing developments, that's no longer practical, particularly if you are interested in catching your horse so you can go for the occasional ride. Domesticating the horse has meant some compromises with his natural state.

One of the most significant changes in the management of the horse, of course, has been in how the horse is fed. Instead of living off the land, most horses are now provided their feed in bags or bales. This means that someone has had to figure out ways to put the feed into those types of packages. Predictably, given people's creative urges, this has given rise to an entire industry.

Still, feeding the horse isn't that difficult. It's a given that all feed contains the same things (see chapter 1), and all horses use those things in the same way (see chapter 2). Plus, there are only so many things you can feed a horse (see chapter 3). So, the only thing that's really left to describe is how the things you can feed a horse are provided for you to buy.

PROCESSED PLANTS

Hays

Hay is made from green plants that are cut down while they are growing, preserved by drying (like jerked meat) and stored to be fed at a later date. Just about any type of plant can be cut and dried and made into hay; the object is to make a good, nutritious feed for the horse. To that end, the object in making good hay is to:

1. Choose a nutritious plant, such as legumes, grasses or cereal crops.
2. Harvest the plants at an optimum stage of maturity so they have maximum nutrient content. (For the most part, hays harvested at "midbloom" are the best choices for horses.)
3. Dry the plants so the moisture content allows them to be stored (and not spoil).

Freshly cut forage is 70 to 85 percent water. Before it can be packaged, forage must be dried to about 20 percent water, which means that after it is cut, fresh forage has to lie in the field and dry out. (If it's not dried prior to being packaged, freshly cut forage will mold, or worse, it will spontaneously catch fire and burn down your barn.)

Drying forage is a bit of a double-edged sword. On the one hand, you can't make hay without drying the grass first. On the other hand, as you dry green plants, nutrients are lost. The amount of nutrient loss increases with the amount of time the forage lies around in the field. This is a particular problem with legume hay because some of the leaves, which are the most nutritious part of the hay, are lost during the drying process. If it happens to rain while the cut plants are trying to dry, that can lead to further leaf loss and increased drying time in the field. In fact, rain-damaged hay can lose as much as 50 to 67 percent of its feeding value.

In addition, as hay dries in the field, if it doesn't get rained on, it gets bleached by the sun. Bleached hay turns from green to brown. The color change may be unsatisfactory from an aesthetic point of view, but more important, sun bleaching causes the hay to lose vitamins. Hay that has lost most of its green color has also lost most of its vitamins. As a rule, the greener the hay, the more vitamins it contains.

Since most of the losses in the nutritional content of hay occur because the fresh plants must be dried, several things can be done to help speed up the drying process. Organic acids, such as propionic acid, can be applied to hay as a preservative. Then the hay can be baled earlier and wetter (at a moisture content of about 30 percent). Unfortunately, horses seem to prefer nontreated hay (even though they can eat hay preserved with propionic acid with no bad effects). Other chemicals, such as potassium carbonate, are hay-drying agents. Drying agents work by dissolving the waxy, waterproof outer layer of the forage stems, which allows the moisture in the plant to escape faster. Hay additives (preservatives and drying agents) increase the cost of hay by a minimum of $10 per ton.

You can't overemphasize the importance of good hay quality. Hay that has mold in it is a potential source of medical problems in a horse. Rodents and rabbits that get caught in the hay-baling equipment are a potential source of botulism. Large round bales, while more economical to feed than smaller bales, are also more easily spoiled because they are often kept outside; they can become a potential source of mold and botulism. Dusty or moldy hay also is a source of irritation to the horse's respiratory tract and has been implicated as a cause of airway problems such as chronic obstructive pulmonary disease. Your veterinary bills will rather quickly offset any savings you make by buying less than good quality hay.

If you think that something's not right with your horse's hay, don't feed it. Hay should look good, and it should smell good. It shouldn't be moldy or excessively dusty. If your hay's not right, take it back to the feed store or hay processor and ask for a replacement.

Haylage and Silage

Hay and grain plants can be cut and stored wet and allowed to ferment in big pits. If proper fermentation steps are taken, haylage and silage are perfectly good feeds. Since they have such a high moisture content, haylage and silage can be great feeds for horses with respiratory problems (such as chronic obstructive pulmonary disease) that are made worse by dusty feeds such as poor hay.

Unfortunately, haylage and silage can mold rather easily if not stored properly. Horses don't do well on moldy feed. Furthermore, haylage and silage have also been implicated as a source of botulism toxicity in horses. In fact, because of the botulism problem, some veterinarians advocate avoiding altogether the use of these feeds in horses, or at least vaccinating against botulism the horses who are to be fed the products.

Hay Cubes

Hay can be rather easily chopped into small pieces and made into cubes. This is done by adding moisture and heat to the chopped hay (by steaming it) and forcing it through a cube die so the pieces of chopped hay stick together. The resultant hay cubes are well accepted by horses once they get used to the fact that they have to eat little bricks of hay instead of the loose feed they are used to.

On the plus side, hay cubes are easy to store, easy to measure and eaten with virtually no waste. If you want to feed your horse twenty pounds of hay cubes, it's most likely going to eat all twenty pounds. (Plus, horses won't pull hay cubes out of the feeder and use it for bedding.) However, even though the hay is chopped up, it has about the same digestibility as loose hay.

On the minus side, horses that eat cubed hay probably don't have as much fun eating as do horses that eat loose hay. As a result, they may tend to get bored and develop fun habits to pass the time, such as weaving in the stall or cribbing. It's also commonly feared that hay cubes will get stuck in the horse's esophagus and cause him to choke; there's no data to support that belief, however.

Some people also seem to think that hay cubes are something of a waste dump for bad hay. This is certainly not the case, although it's true that you can't see the hay that went into the cubes. Feed manufacturers would not stay in business if their product were detrimental to your horse's health. There's really nothing inherently wrong with feeding a horse hay cubes (and there are some good reasons for doing so).

Processed Grains

Whole Unfortified Grains

Whole grains are the seed heads of a plant that are harvested from the field and dried to a suitable moisture content for storage. Such grains include oats, corn, barley, wheat and milo. Unfortunately, with the single exception of oats, whole grains are not the best choice to give to horses. This is because the grains have a hard outer hull that protects the starch portion of the grain; consequently, it's very difficult for the horse to digest most whole grains in its small intestine. In addition, the type of starch found in most whole grains is not easily digested by the small intestine of the horse. As a result, most grains should be mechanically processed prior to feeding them to the horse.

Processed, Unfortified Grains

There are many different ways in which grain can be mechanically processed. All of these ways break the grain kernel apart. Breaking apart the

· FIGURE 2 ·

grain kernel increases the surface area of the grain that's available for the chemicals and enzymes of the digestive process to work on. Some common methods of processing grains include:

- *Cracking* Breaking the kernel into two or more pieces (done particularly with corn).
- *Crimping* Slightly flattening the grain (done particularly with small grains, such as oats).
- *Flaking* Treating the grain with heat and/or moisture and then flattening it.
- *Grinding* Forcing the grain between rollers or through sized screens.
- *Rolling* Smashing grain with corrugated rollers operating at different speeds. This can be done with or without steam treatment of the grain.

Processing grains doesn't increase the amount of nutrients that the horse can get from grain. The point of processing grains is to enable the starch to be digested in the small intestine rather than in the hindgut. Even though the horse can digest grains in the hindgut, that's not ideally where it should be done (for reasons mentioned in chapter 2). In general, processing grains will increase the small intestinal digestibility by 10 to 30 percent, depending on the grain. The benefits are well worth the extra cost.

Processed, Fortified Grains

Processed, fortified grains are among the products most commonly fed to horses. These grains have been subjected to some form of processing and have been supplemented with a vitamin and mineral package. The added vitamins and minerals are provided to feed manufacturers by special companies known as *premix manufacturers*. Premix manufacturers have high-tech mixing systems that allow them to mix very accurately small amounts of material. The finished vitamin and mineral packages are a combination of small amounts of many ingredients. Usually both fat- and water-soluble vitamins and trace minerals are included in these premixes. Major minerals such as sodium and chloride (salt), calcium and phosphorus are needed in large enough quantities. They are added by the feed manufacturer at the time of mixing.

Blending grains with vitamin and mineral supplements requires a feed mixer. Feed mixers allow feed manufacturers to do all sorts of fun things to grain products and give you even more choices for feeding your horse. Typically, two or more types of processed grains (such as corn and oats) are mixed together in these products. Mixing grain products can have some advantages. For example, individual grains have a certain protein and amino acid profile. If you mix oats with soybean meal, the amount and quality of the protein is increased over that provided in oats alone. Similarly, the mixture of corn and oats provides more energy on an equal weight basis than does feeding oats alone.

Textured "Sweet" Feeds

Sweet feeds are typically made up of a mix of several grains blended with a light coating of molasses and occasionally vegetable oil. The result is a moist, sort of sticky mix often called a "sweet" feed. The ingredients in these feeds are easy to identify; you get some sense of ingredient quality when you look at them. Plus, sweet feeds smell good and give you the impression that you are feeding your horse well. From a nutritional standpoint, however, sweet feeds don't offer any advantage over any other type of grain product that you can feed your horse (but horses usually dive right into the stuff).

Pellets

Feed can also be made into small, hard pellets. First the feed is ground mechanically. Then the resultant mash is conditioned with moisture, heat

(180 degrees Fahrenheit) and pressure and forced into a pellet-sized diemold. The pellets are then cooled and sent through screens to remove broken pellets and finer particles. The finished pellets are put into bags or stored in bulk bins for delivery.

Just about any type of feed can be pelleted. Most of the same advantages and disadvantages that apply to cubed hay apply also to pelleted hay. (See chapter 11, "Feed Myths," for more information on pelleted feeds.) Hays can be mixed with grains and made into a pellet, too. Pellets made from hay and grain have more energy in them than do pellets made from hay alone. Of course, pellets made from grain alone have even more energy. Making grain into pellets also helps it get digested in the small intestine where it belongs.

One advantage of pelleted feeds is that they can be easily stored (bags of hay pellets don't take up nearly as much space as a bale of hay) and that they are eaten with very little waste. If you live where winters get cold, sweet feeds containing molasses turn into frozen blocks, but pelleted concentrates won't.

Extruded Feeds

If you have a dog, a cat or some fish, you've seen extruded feeds. Some of the food you eat has been extruded (corn chips, for example). The process of extrusion is somewhat similar to that of pelleting; however, when feed is extruded, the heat is so intense (about 250 degrees Fahrenheit) that it is actually cooked.

The intense heat and pressure associated with the extrusion process actually alter the physical makeup of the feed. This allows the manufacturer to form the feed into different shapes (although horse feed manufacturers are not nearly as creative as those who make pet food; extruded horse feed looks pretty much like little rocks).

Cooking feed before giving it to your horse has several advantages. Cooking totally exposes the starch granules in the feed to digestion. As a result, the digestibility of extruded feeds is slightly higher than that of pellets. Horses tend to eat extruded feeds more slowly and generally are not able to gulp the stuff down. You can add all sorts of things to extruded feed, including a higher amount of fat than can be added to grain mixes. The shelf life of the products is also excellent. (Have you ever seen moldy dog food?)

Extruded feed also has some disadvantages. Vitamins can be lost in the high heat of processing. As you might expect, all the processing required to make extruded feed also jacks up the cost. Also, it can be hard to get horses to eat the feeds, at least initially. Whether the cost of the feed is worth the benefits is a decision you have to make for yourself. Furthermore, the availability of extruded feeds is somewhat limited; the products are not made in many parts of the world.

FEED QUALITY

Horse feed, like the food in your refrigerator, is perishable. This is primarily related to the amount of moisture in the feed (you've probably noticed that moist bread will mold whereas crackers won't). It's also related to where you live; food will spoil a lot more quickly in a warm, moist environment than it will in a cool, dry one.

Hay can be kept for a long time. If it is dried properly prior to baling and stored so as to protect it from the weather and sunlight, hay can be stored in a barn for at least a year. Some of the vitamin content of the hay may decrease with storage (especially vitamins A and E) but the energy, protein and mineral content is well preserved. Thus, as a general rule, if you have enough storage space, you can buy hay once a year. If you don't have a huge hay barn, you can usually buy hay in smaller quantities. However, this doesn't mean that the hay you buy will necessarily be fresher; since hay production is seasonal in most places, somebody has had to store the hay that you buy in the off-season.

Grains are also perishable. Whole, unprocessed grains have the greatest shelf life. Grain production—like hay—is seasonal, and whole grains can be harvested, dried and stored for over a year. Once grain gets processed, however, it's shelf life begins to decrease dramatically. Thus, grain companies don't routinely store processed grains. Grains are usually processed immediately before being mixed in feed. Most grain elevators and feed stores rotate their grain inventory, trying to have the products to the consumer within one month of production.

Processed grains that are made into pelleted or extruded feeds and feeds that have less than 4 percent molasses have a shelf life of about six months after they are produced. Feeds with more than 4 percent molasses or with more than 3.5 percent fat are more prone to spoilage and have a shelf life of about three months. Of course, once you buy a grain product, it has to be properly stored to live up to the shelf-life expectations. Grain should be stored in sealed containers that resist moisture accumulation and keep out things like sunlight and marauding rodents. As a general rule, you shouldn't purchase grain for your horse that isn't going to be fed within 30 days after you buy it. Many feed manufacturers are starting to help you buy fresh feed by putting "feed by" dates on the bags.

If you give your horse the appropriate amounts of good quality, fresh feed, its nutritional needs will be satisfied. However, there is a peculiar human desire to tinker so as to make things "better" (this could also be described as an inability to leave well enough alone). Thus, in addition to giving your horse feed, you can give it lots of supplements. Those are the subjects of the next chapter.

Chapter 5

Feed Supplements

By definition, a supplement is something that is provided to "complete something, to make up for a deficiency or to extend and strengthen the whole" (*American Heritage Dictionary of the English Language*). Supplements are usually given to horses to help make up for perceived deficiencies in their diets or to generally "make them better." Whether you want the horse's hooves to be harder, the hair to be shinier, the "jump" to be higher or the horse to feel more at ease in his surroundings, there's likely to be some supplement advertised that will claim to help you do it.

Frankly, the most common thing lacking in most horses' diets is energy; without enough calories in its diet, the horse is going to lose weight and/or not be able to perform to its expected level. Of course, finding out that your horse's performance or weight problem is related to an inadequate amount of feed is sort of like finding out that your television set wasn't working because it wasn't plugged in. You're happy to find out what the problem is, but it's really kind of embarrassing and you'd really rather it be something else. Nonetheless, rather than sit down and evaluate the caloric needs of their horse and then supply what's needed, many owners with performance or weight-related problems run down to the feed store and buy some supplement in an effort to "help."

The stuff you can add to your horse's feed usually fits into one of two categories. Either it is stuff that is required in the horse's diet in some form (such as protein, vitamins or minerals) or it is stuff for which there is no known nutritional need but for which a lot of theoretical benefits are suggested (such as everything else). It's actually kind of hard to make a diet that's deficient in the stuff that is required, as long as your horse is being fed enough good-quality feed to maintain his weight (please note the reappearance of the term "good quality"). As for the other stuff, this book will give you a lot of information so you can make up your own mind.

Supplements apparently are often given in an effort to "improve" or "strengthen" the horse. This generally means that the supplement is given because the owner wants the horse to be somehow better or different than it actually is (a problem that plagues many relationships). Supplements claim to do such things as "Improve the overall bloom," "Better general health" or "Increase mental stability" (whatever those phrases mean). In fact, since these concepts are so vague and "improvement" is such a subjective concept (how much credit do you give a feed supplement for a "68" instead of a "66" on a dressage test?), they are impossible to measure (or even define).

Many supplements are promoted by stating what the supplement's individual ingredients are and how they are used in the horse. Then, either directly or indirectly, horse owners are led to believe that their horses may not be getting enough of those ingredients. For example, the statement, "This supplement contains 14 essential amino acids. If any one of them is deficient in your horse's diet, his protein needs may not be fulfilled," is undoubtedly true. However, amino acid–deficient diets have never been reported in the mature horse. Similar examples can be given for vitamins, minerals and electrolytes, other commonly supplemented substances in the horse's diet.

Apparently, another line of thinking for supplying supplements is, "If some is good, more is better." This isn't necessarily so. For example, while it can be absolutely demonstrated that a horse has a requirement in his diet for many vitamins, giving the horse more vitamins than it needs doesn't help; in fact, vitamin toxicities from overzealous supplementation have been described in horses. It just doesn't make any sense to supply stuff to your horse willy-nilly in hopes that you're doing something good.

Frankly, it's highly unlikely that you could hurt your horse by supplying it with any number of the available over-the-counter supplements , as long as you follow the recommendations of the manufacturer (hurting your pocketbook is another matter). Nonetheless, since you are undoubtedly going to wonder about the maze of supplement products that will confront you upon entering any feed store, this chapter gives you some guidance as to what you are actually buying (and what you can expect from the products).

PROTEIN

While protein is unquestionably an important component of the horse's diet (see chapter 2), extra protein is rarely necessary for a normal horse. The only time additional protein becomes really important in a horse's diet is when the horse is growing (see chapter 8). While things like heavy exercise, pregnancy and lactation do slightly increase the requirement for protein in the horse, the fact that you are going to have to give these horses more feed to take care of their extra energy requirements will usually take care of their need for extra protein.

If you do add extra protein to your horse's diet, you're not going to hurt it. Extra protein in the diet is simply used as a source of energy. Unfortunately, (at least from a metabolic standpoint), protein is not a particularly good source of energy; it requires a lot of metabolic work to get energy from protein (that's what's generally meant when people refer to a feed as being "difficult to digest"). Protein supplements are among the more expensive supplements that you can buy, so unless you just like to spend money on expensive things that have little purpose (you know who you are), there's little reason to add protein supplements to the diets of most horses.

VITAMINS AND MINERALS

While no one seems to keep statistics on this sort of thing, asserting that vitamins and minerals are likely the most frequently supplemented item in the horse's diet would hardly raise eyebrows. Given that horses definitely need them, that deficiencies of various vitamins and minerals can be produced experimentally and that the experimental diets can be shown to be bad for the horse's health, adding vitamins and minerals to the horse's diet seems to be perceived as a "good" thing to do.

The biggest problem with giving supplemental vitamins and minerals to horses is that most of the time they're a waste of time and money. Feeding good-quality feed to a horse usually provides for all its vitamin and mineral needs. Once again, the phrase "good quality" is important here; poor-quality feed may indeed be vitamin or mineral deficient (you shouldn't be feeding your horse poor feed anyway). Additionally, if you feed your horse commercially produced grain products that come in bags, vitamins and minerals are added to them; giving even more vitamins and minerals is a duplication of nutritional effort. (If you feed unfortified grain products along with your hay, it is possible that your horse's diet will be deficient in some minerals.)

However, perhaps the main reason vitamin and mineral supplements are generally a waste of time is that they usually don't contain significant amounts of vitamins and minerals. Horses are big creatures. Accordingly, they need big amounts of things. If you add up the quantities of vitamins and minerals the horse needs in his diet, you come up with about a pound of stuff. You just can't fit the vitamin and mineral requirements of a horse into a scoopful that weighs an ounce or two. Many vitamin and mineral supplements for the horse contain as much as 1 to 3 percent of the daily requirements of some vitamins and minerals; while these amounts are too small to make much of an impression in the horse's diet, providing supplements with such minimal amounts of the desired components can definitely make a significant dent in your pocketbook!

That said, in specific conditions and in appropriate amounts, vitamin and mineral supplementation can be appropriate in the horse. It can also be inappropriate; toxicities (poisonings) of some vitamins and minerals have also been reported in the horse. Thus, it's probably useful to look briefly at some of the vitamins and minerals supplemented to the horse and at the reasons for which they are provided.

- *Vitamin A*   If a horse ever has an opportunity to eat forage that contains the color green, then it most likely gets sufficient quantities of vitamin A. Clinical signs of vitamin A deficiencies have only been seen in diets that are experimentally produced to be lacking in the vitamin. However, recent research suggests that horses kept on a diet consisting solely of hay may become marginal in their vitamin A levels; it may be advisable to provide some additional vitamin A in the diets of these horses. (Just about any vitamin-fortified feed product will do.) There have been occasional reports of vitamin A toxicities from oversupplementation. The signs of deficiencies in vitamin A are similar to those of vitamin A toxicity and include dry skin, night blindness, excessive tear formation and decreased reproductive efficiency.

- *B vitamins* It's virtually impossible to make a horse deficient in B vitamins, as long as you feed it. However, B-vitamin preparations are frequently given to horses for a variety of reasons. Injections of vitamin B complex are often given as an appetite stimulant; research has failed to demonstrate any effect in this regard. *Thiamine* (Vitamin B_1) has been used as a "natural" tranquilizer; again, no consistent effects have been demonstrated in research done on this proposed effect. Furthermore, thiamine injections are forbidden by the governing bodies of virtually all performance horse organizations; also, severe allergic reactions after the intravenous use of thiamine have been reported. Vitamin B_{12} is often given in an effort to "pep up" a horse or to increase its red blood cell production; again, experiments have failed to show any effect in this regard. Furthermore, injected vitamin B_{12} is rapidly removed from the horse's body by the liver and kidneys. Finally, folic acid supplementation, although not necessary in normal horses, may occasionally be prescribed for the treatment of horses with *equine protozoal myelitis* (EPM), described in chapter 10).
- *Biotin* This is commonly added to a horse's feed to promote hoof quality. Initial investigations done on pigs suggested that supplementation with biotin improved hoof quality in that species. Subsequently, several studies done on horses suggest that biotin can help improve the resiliency and quality of the hoof in some horses. The hoof grows from the coronary band down to the ground. Biotin can only be incorporated into the hoof at the growth level, where the hoof is still live tissue. Therefore, several months may elapse before any effect from biotin supplementation is seen in the horse's hoof. Unfortunately, biotin doesn't help every horse with bad feet. Recommended doses of biotin for horses with hoof problems have ranged from 15 to 30 milligrams per day; neither biotin toxicity nor biotin deficiencies have been reported in the horse.

- *Vitamin C*   Neither vitamin C deficiencies nor toxicities have ever been reported in the horse. Since horses make all the vitamin C they need, there's no apparent reason to give them any more of it.
- *Vitamin D*   Since vitamin D is produced in the skin upon exposure to sunlight, it's pretty hard to make a horse deficient in vitamin D. It can be done experimentally by feeding growing horses diets deficient in the vitamin and keeping them inside (but why would you ever do that to *your* horse?). Deficiencies in vitamin D show up as abnormalities of bone growth (called rickets). Vitamin D toxicities have been reported, mostly in association with horses that eat the wild jasmine plant (*Cestrum diurnum*), although there have been occasional reports of vitamin D toxicities from over-supplementation. The signs of vitamin D toxicosis include stiffness and soreness, lack of eating, weight loss, excessive drinking and urination and calcification of the kidneys. Vitamin D toxicity usually means the end of the road for the horse.
- *Vitamin E*   In addition to its important bodily functions, vitamin E is also an antioxidant. Antioxidant compounds help to keep things from deteriorating when they are exposed to oxygen (as can occur in the process of inflammation). For this reason, vitamin E is commonly used (often in combination with the mineral selenium) in the treatment of horses with exertional rhabdomyolysis ("tying up"; see chapter 10). Vitamin E deficiencies have also been implicated as a cause of an unusual condition called *equine motor neuron disease* (EMN), also covered in chapter 10.
- *Vitamin K*   Vitamin K deficiencies are unknown in the horse.
- *Calcium*   Adding supplemental calcium to a mature, nonpregnant horse's diet is rarely, if ever, required. Legume hays have high amounts of calcium in them, far more than is needed by the horse; even grass or grain hays, while much lower in calcium than the

legume hays, still supply ample calcium (assuming that the horse gets enough hay to eat). Added calcium is a part of processed, vitamin- and mineral-fortified grain concentrates as well. Most horses are exposed to a lot of calcium in their regular diet; it's unusual to find a situation in which they would need more (one such instance is cited in the next paragraph, however).

- *Phosphorus*   Additional phosphorus is typically given to horses that exist on diets consisting of primarily legume hays like alfalfa. To some extent, that's not a bad idea; however, feeding too much phosphorus causes the body to lose calcium. As mentioned in the last chapter, overfeeding phosphorus results in a condition called "big head" (the medical term is *nutritional secondary hyperparathyroidism*). "Big head" is an almost unheard of condition in the United States. However, in other countries, nutritional secondary hyperparathyroidism can also be seen when horses eat grasses that are high in chemicals known as *oxalates,* such as setaria, green or blue panic, argentine or Dallis grass and buffel grasses. In these cases, there's not enough calcium available to balance out the phosphorus; the oxalate ties up dietary calcium and prevents it from being absorbed. (You have to either remove the oxalate or give the horse more calcium if you want to avoid this problem.)

- *Copper*   Supplemental copper has been advocated to aid in the prevention of osteochondrosis, a developmental disease of young, growing horses (that's discussed in chapter 10). There's some emerging research that suggests that feeding pregnant mares supplemental copper may be even more effective than feeding the foals in helping to prevent developmental abnormalities.

- *Zinc*   Although they do not appear to be very common, zinc deficiencies may be associated with poor-quality feeds. Zinc deficiencies show up first in the hooves and hair. Zinc toxicities have been reported where pastures have been contaminated due to metal smelting activity or water has been contaminated from porous galvanized pipe. Zinc toxicity affects the bones and joints, and causes affected horses to be stiff and lame and to have swollen joints.

- *Selenium* Selenium deficiencies can be seen in areas where the soil lacks selenium, particularly in some areas of the Great Lakes region and the Eastern, Gulf and Northwestern coastal areas of the United States. "White muscle disease" is a selenium deficiency of foals characterized by muscle weakness and listlessness.

  Selenium toxicities can also occur; these are mostly seen in horses that eat plants that accumulate selenium, in areas such as the Rocky Mountain or Great Plains states. Selenium toxicity shows up mostly as signs of lameness (that can be confused with laminitis, an inflammatory condition of the horse's feet), rough and brittle hair coat and swelling of the coronary band.

Other Trace Minerals

Most horses are given trace minerals and/or salt either in a block they can lick or chew or sprinkled on top of their feed. The salt may be important; the trace minerals may not be. Salt blocks or loose salt preparations that also contain trace minerals actually contain very little in the way of trace minerals. If your horse gets enough of the trace minerals zinc, copper and selenium, (which are commonly added in vitamin- and mineral-fortified grain concentrates), it's probably getting plenty of the other trace minerals, too.

ELECTROLYTES (BODY SALTS)

The dissolved body salts in the horse's system conduct the electricity that runs the horse's body (for example, you can measure the electrical impulses in the horse's beating heart). There's no question that ample levels of dietary electrolytes are critical for the horse's normal body function at all times.

Fortunately, making sure that horses have enough electrolytes usually isn't that big a deal. Horses get exposed to a lot of salt in their environment and can ingest plenty of electrolytes by doing such things as licking dirt. Feeds such as vitamin- and mineral-fortified grains are generally loaded with salts. Plus, most horse owners stick a salt block or loose salt (with or without trace minerals) in the horse's feeder "just in case." It's usually not necessary to provide anything else.

In rare instances, however, additional electrolyte supplementation may be beneficial for a horse that exercises heavily in hot weather. Horse sweat contains lots of electrolytes. It is therefore possible to make a horse sweat out a significant portion of its electrolytes by riding it hard in hot weather without stopping to give it rest or water. In fact, research has shown that providing water, glucose and electrolytes to endurance horses does seem to delay the onset of fatigue. However, routine supplementation of electrolytes beyond what is normally provided in the diet is clearly not needed, even in the hottest weather, in most normal working horses.

YEAST

As pointed out in chapter 2, the horse normally digests protein, fat, nonstructural carbohydrates, vitamins and minerals in the small intestine. These components of feed are almost completely digested; thus, there's little room to improve their digestibility. However, the hindgut, into which gets dumped all the fiber, may be another matter. Fiber digestion is accomplished by the action of the bacteria that live in the large intestine; it's at least reasonable to hope that you could help the bacteria do their job.

One way to try to do this is to add yeast cultures to the horse's diet. Yeast doesn't normally live in the horse's hindgut because the intestinal environment isn't ideal (the pH is too high). Adding yeast to a horse's diet has been shown to increase fiber digestion by about 8 percent and to improve the digestion of the mineral phosphorus by about 20 to 25 percent. That's probably not enough of an increase to make a significant difference in a normal horse, but it is something to consider if you have a horse who has difficulty gaining or keeping weight.

BACTERIA

As you know, there are bacteria living throughout your horse's intestinal tract that help with the digestive process. (Of course, not all bacteria are such good fellows; bacteria can also cause many serious diseases.) In the spirit of "if some is good, more is better," some clever person got the idea of putting some of the good digestive bacteria (generally some type of *Lactobacillus* or *Streptococcus* species) into a tube of paste, a dried powder or a big pill so that it can be given to horses. These products are often referred to as "probiotics."

The bacteria in these tubes is in a state of suspended animation, much as is the dry yeast you use when you bake bread. To keep them quiet, the bacteria are packaged with very little water and coated with a gum coating. The coating dissolves in the digestive tract, allowing the bacteria to become active.

Oral bacterial supplements are commonly given to newborn foals and to adult horses with diarrhea or perceived digestive problems (like a failure to gain weight). Whether these products actually do anything is a bit of a question; although you can find lots of people who use them, there really aren't any veterinary studies to indicate that they are effective therapies.

A recent study in human medicine concluded that not enough is known about the normal bacteria that live in the human intestines to be able to make realistic assessments about the effects of putting in more bacteria. It's very much the same way in horses.

ENZYMES

Enzyme preparations that help the digestion of carbohydrates are often added to the diets of poultry and, to a lesser extent, swine. There are specific enzymes used to digest specific grains, and research has shown that they are useful in helping digestive efficiency in poultry. Although they are out there, there's really not much information available about the use of enzyme preparations in horses. Given that horses usually don't eat that much grain (relative to their forage intake) and they're really good at digesting what they get, the use of enzyme preparations in horses doesn't seem to have much of a place.

HERBS

There appears to be great interest in "natural" products for human health. Thus, it should come as no great surprise that there are natural products available for horses as well.

There are herbal products available for horses that purport to help maintain the health of the horse's digestive tract. While there's no question that many drugs used in medicine come from a plant or herb origin—when herbs do have an effect, it's because they have active substances (drugs) in them. The problem with plants and herbs is that the amount of active substances that occur in them varies tremendously from plant to plant. As a result, you don't necessarily know what you're getting when you buy a bucket of herbs. Plus, there's really no research to indicate that herbs have any significant beneficial effects in horses. Thus, it's a bit silly to assert that just throwing a bunch of herbs to your horse is going to be of benefit to its health.

Of course not all "natural" substances are benign, either. There are numerous naturally occuring toxic plants that can cause all sorts of problems for horses. That's not to say that the herbal products you can buy for your horse are likely to do any harm—there's just no good evidence that they will do much good.

CHROMIUM

Chromium is a trace mineral for which there is no known dietary requirement in the horse. It's only known function is to help increase the action of the hormone insulin, which helps direct the flow of nutrients to various tissues of the horse. Research in humans and pigs has shown that chromium helps to increase the deposition of lean muscle and reduces body fat.

Experiments in horses supplemented with chromium in their diet showed that they had lower insulin levels than did nonsupplemented horses (suggesting that less insulin was needed to get the nutrients into the horse). Lactic acid, which accumulates during exercise and is thought to be one factor that contributes to fatigue, was reduced. So was plasma cortisol, which is used as a measurement of stress. The experimental results suggest that chromium supplementation might be useful in a highly stressed performance horse.

There's no way to determine whether your horse is lacking in chromium. Most mature horses that are used for pleasure or showing probably don't need it. Strenuous exercise and/or diets that have a lot of grain in them increase the excretion of chromium into the horse's urine, however, so horses in heavy training or fast-growing horses that eat a lot of grain are potential candidates for chromium supplementation. It's also been suggested that chromium be used to treat horses with exertional rhabdomyolysis (tying up) because of chromium's action on insulin (but some research in that area would be helpful before it could be routinely recommended). Chromium supplementation is currently not approved for supplementation of horses in the United States and must be prescribed by a veterinarian.

DIMETHYLGLYCINE (DMG)

DMG is a substance that occurs naturally in many foods. It is supposed to increase the utilization of oxygen and decrease the production of lactic acid by the muscles during high-intensity exercise (lactic acid, a by-product of muscle metabolism, rises as muscles get tired).

Several studies on DMG in people have shown that it does not have any consistent effects. The studies done on horses have shown some conflicting results, but the most recent study concluded that exercising horses given DMG had no improvement in the oxygen-carrying capacity of their blood. Nor was there any change in lactic acid concentration in the plasma, blood or muscle in this study.

In horses, DMG has most commonly been promoted as a substance to help reduce the incidence of tying up. There's no scientific evidence to suggest that DMG would actually do this. Furthermore, the mechanism by which DMG would exert a beneficial effect on horses that tie up is somewhat unclear since an increase in lactic acid production (at least as measured in the blood) does not appear to be a feature of this disease.

HYDROXYMETHYL BUTYRATE (HMB)

ß-hydroxy-ß-methylbutyrate (HMB) is a normal product made in the muscle tissue from the amino acid leucine. Once HMB is formed, it serves as a building block for the formation of cholesterol in the muscle. During stressful situations, like heavy training and exercise, it is theorized that the muscle cell may not be able to make enough cholesterol for maximal growth or function. Supplying HMB to the diet supposedly would keep blood cholesterol at an optimal level. Work in humans has indicated that aerobic exercise performance and muscular strength are improved with HMB supplementation.

A recent treadmill study with Quarter Horses and a experiment on the track with Thoroughbreds conducted by researchers at Iowa State University provides some interesting information about HMB. If you look carefully at the research, it appears that statistically there were no differences between HMB-supplemented and control horses (on both treadmill and at the track). There were, however, noticeable improvements in many aspects of exercise performance in the study. For instance, there was a 5 percent increase in red blood cells ($P < .09$), 46 percent lower CK levels ($P < .07$), a 15 percent decrease in other muscle-related enzymes (NS) and a higher win rate on the track (18.8 percent HMB versus 11.4 percent controls). Although the test groups of 24 horses each were fairly large (according to typical equine research) the large variation found in horses makes it difficult to know just exactly what to make of the supplement. Furthermore, it has not yet been proven that orally supplemented HMB actually reaches the muscle cell intact.

CARNITINE

Carnitine's normal function is to help the horse's body use fatty acids. Thus, it has a very important role in metabolism, especially during exercise. It has been shown that you can increase the amount of carnitine running around in the horse's blood by feeding the horse carnitine. However, the same study showed that carnitine levels weren't increased in the muscle, which is where it would have to be in order to work. There isn't any evidence that giving carnitine to a horse will help increase or improve its exercise performance. In human studies, the results of carnitine supplementation have been conflicting.

COENZYME Q10

Coenzyme Q10 also has an important function in metabolism during exercise; however, giving extra COENZYME Q10 doesn't appear to have any effect on blood measurements of exercise efficiency in at least one study on horses. Work in humans suggests that COENZYME Q10 doesn't help them either.

CREATINE

Creatine is yet another important player in the game of energy metabolism. In humans, giving extra creatine in the diet has been shown to increase creatine in the muscle (where it would have to be in order to work). It has also been reported as improving the performance of some types of exercise. In humans, very short-term, high intensity exercise seems to benefit some from creatine supplementation but continuous exercise does not. Even though the effects of giving creatine to horses have not been reported, it seems that very few horses participate in the type of exercise activity that would be helped by giving them extra creatine in their diet.

OCTOCOSANOL

Octocosanol is an alcohol that is found in some vegetable oils and waxes, most notably in wheat germ oil. It has been promoted as a supplement that can improve performance and work output in the horse.

It is supposed to increase oxygen transport by the body. How it might do so is unclear, however.

The consensus of results on studies of octocosanol in humans is that it does not improve endurance. Its purported benefits have certainly never been proven in the horse.

There are lots of other things you can feed to your horse that have no particular nutritional value. For example, chondroitin sulfate and glucosamine hydrochloride are marketed as "nutraceutical" products that may have beneficial effects in horse joints (the jury is still out; there's a lot of information on these products in the *Concise Guide to Arthritis in the Horse*).

Before feeding any sort of supplement to your horse, you should do two things. First, discuss with an expert whether any particular additional nutrients are needed by horses in your area (a nutritionist, agricultural extension agent or a veterinarian might be a good place to start). Regional changes in the nutrient content of horse feed may make the addition of some supplements of value. If your horse needs additional calcium, phosphorus, copper, zinc (or whatever), it needs to be added *specifically* to its diet. Second, read the label of your feed or feed supplement and find out what the ingredients are. Look for specific product information about things that your horse may be lacking in its diet, and ignore vague and sometimes outrageous claims of effectiveness. After all, just because somebody has something to sell you doesn't mean that you should buy it.

CHAPTER 6

The Ground Rules

In many ways, feeding your horse is like driving to an unknown destination using a road map. There are lots of different roads that can take you to your intended destination. The "best" route for getting somewhere is decided on by using a combination of factors such as how frequently you want to stop, whether you like taking the scenic route and the mood the kids are in. Similarly, the "best" way to feed your horse can be a matter of how many products you want to buy (your road stops), how much you like to fuss with your horse's diet (the scenic route) and whether the horse will eat what you feed it (the mood of the kids).

Still, even though you have choices in your driving route, there are certain rules you have to follow. You have to put gas in the car, you must stop at red lights and so on. There are feed rules, too. However, once you understand what you can feed your horse and what your horse must have in its diet, actually feeding the horse becomes mostly a matter of knowing what you want. If you have well-defined goals as to what you want out of your horse (from a nutritional standpoint), you can fairly easily choose feed items that might help you get there.

GETTING STARTED

Before you get going on the specific information about how to feed your particular horse, you might want to consider a couple of things. First of all, to get any sort of realistic idea at all about how much and what you should be feeding your horse, you should try to get some idea of what he weighs. There are several ways you can do this:

1. You can weigh him on a scale. Unfortunately, this isn't necessarily the easiest thing to do, since most scales that are big enough to accommodate a horse are usually found only at places that service big trucks.

2. You can eyeball him. Unfortunately, this isn't all that great an option, unless you've got a lot of experience actually weighing horses. In fact, research has shown that most people significantly overestimate the weight of their horses.

3. You can use a weight tape. Weight tapes can be obtained from a variety of sources (feed stores, catalogues and the like). They are calibrated to give you an estimate of your horse's weight based on the distance measured around his barrel at the withers (the heart girth circumference). Although weight tapes are not particularly precise, they can provide a reasonably good estimate of the horse's weight, and they are very useful for monitoring weight gains and losses.

4. To get an estimate you can use the scale provided here, which uses a combination of two measurements (see figures 3a and 3b).

The second thing you should do is get used to the idea of weighing your horse's feed. "Flakes" of hay and "coffee cans" of grain are not very accurate measurements (although they are very convenient). If you weigh your horse's feed, using any type of scale that will fit in your tack room or shed, you'll be able to accurately provide what your horse needs in his feed. Plus, it will save you a lot of money in the long run because you won't be wasting feed on your horse. Once you get used to measuring your horse's feed, it becomes almost second nature (really).

FEED RULES

Like any other game, feeding your horse has certain well-defined rules. You can do a lot of different things while playing the game, but you have to follow the hard and fast rules or your horse will suffer for it. Fortunately, there aren't very many rules that you have to remember—just these seven:

1. The majority of your horse's diet must be made up of forage. That is, your horse's diet has to consist mostly of either pasture, hay or hay products (like pellets and cubes). That's the way a horse is and you can't do anything about it.

2. Your horse should always have unlimited access to clean, fresh water.

3. You should always feed good-quality feed. Poor-quality feed may be lacking in virtually everything that feed is supposed to provide your horse. Things like mold, dust and foreign material, which can contaminate hay, are not good for your horse's health. If you don't care enough about your horse to feed it the best feed that's available, sell your horse or find a good home for it. What's the point of keeping a horse if you're not going to take care of it?

4. If your horse needs extra energy, provide it. That doesn't just mean that you throw in more hay. It may not be possible to give your horse enough hay to fulfill the energy demands you make of it. Hay takes up a lot of room in the horse's stomach. Horses can fill up on hay and not be physically able to get enough of it to meet

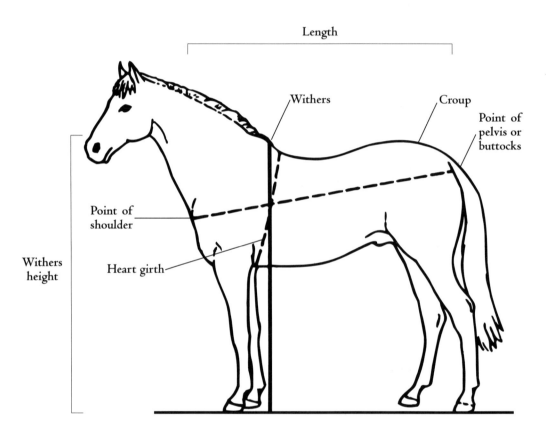

Step one in estimating your horse's weight is to measure the girth and length, as shown here.

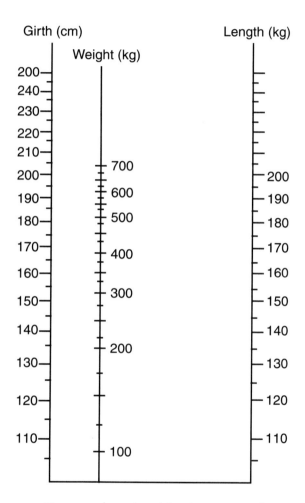

After you take girth and length, use a straight edge to connect the appropriate side of this chart. Your horse's estimated weight is the point where the ruler crosses the weight scale (1kg = 2.2 lbs).

their energy requirements if they are exercising heavily, breeding or growing. You may have to provide your horse extra energy in the form of grain and/or fat.

5. If you feed your horse grain, never feed him more than five pounds (approximately 2.25 kilos) at one feeding. This is because of the relatively small size of the horse's stomach and to avoid the potential complications associated with lots of undigested starch getting into the hindgut (refer to chapter 2).

6. Feed regularly, at least twice a day.

7. If you make dietary changes for your horse, do them slowly, over a period of a couple of weeks (among other reasons, this is to help prevent colic).

Now that you know and understand the ground rules, you should be able to come up with some good ideas about how to feed your particular horse. You'll get plenty of help and suggestions with that in the next chapters.

CHAPTER 7

Feeding Your Horse
For Maintenance

To feed any horse, you have to have a starting point. That starting point does not take into account whether you want your horse to gain weight, to exercise regularly or to have a baby (all of which require extra nutrients). The starting point is the amount of feed you must feed your horse to keep it alive, without losing any weight. It is the amount of feed needed to maintain your horse in good health.

It is generally possible to maintain your horse's weight with a diet that consists only of good-quality forage, water, salt and possibly a trace mineral supplement (depending on the quality of the forage). As a minimum starting point, you can figure that your horse will need about 1.5 percent of its body weight in forage to maintain its weight. That is, if your horse weighs 1,000 pounds, it will need at least 15 pounds of feed per day to keep from losing weight (a 500kg horse would need 7.5 kilos of feed in this example). Your horse may be able to do just fine on hay alone; some horses need hay and grain. However, of the amount of feed you give your horse, an absolute minimum of two-thirds of it must be forage (10 of the 15 pounds in this example). Some horses need more feed than this; some horses just seem to be able to eat and eat and not gain any weight. (You have friends like this, and you hate them, too.) But the 1.5 percent figure is a good one to keep in mind.

In addition to enough feed to provide energy, the horse being fed for maintenance needs unlimited access to water. Most people also will allow the horse unlimited access to trace mineral salt. If you're in an area where the forage is mineral deficient or of poor quality, you may need to consider supplementing some specific vitamins and minerals as well.

HOW MUCH SHOULD MY HORSE WEIGH?

After you've decided how much your horse weighs and how much to feed it, you need to get some idea of how much it should weigh. Horses (like people) come in a variety of shapes and sizes. Still, the "ideal" body condition for a horse is described as the weight where you can't see the horse's ribs, but you can feel them easily. This is not a hard-and-fast rule. Some horses, like race horses, polo horses and horses used in endurance events are kept a little on the lean side. Other horses, such as show hunters or dressage horses, in whom a hint of rib suggests to owners and trainers that the horse is being starved, are kept a little fatter than the "ideal" condition.

To help you figure out the condition your horse is in, here's a "Condition Score" from 1 to 9 that you can use to rate your horse—adapted from D. R. Henneke, "Relationship Between Condition Score, Physical Measurement and Body Fat Percentage in Mares," Equine Veterinary Journal, 15 (1983): 371—as well as some drawings of horses of various body conditions (see figure 4, a condensed version of the Condition Score list):

1. **Poor** Extremely emaciated; spinous processes, ribs, tailhead, tuber coxae and ischii project prominently; bone structure of withers, shoulders and neck easily noticeable; no fatty tissue can be felt.

· FIGURE 4 ·

Very Poor

Poor

Moderate

Good

Fat

Obese

Examples of different body types.

(These poor horses can tread water in a garden hose or run through a harp and not strike a note.)

2. **Very thin**   Emaciated; slight fat covering over base of spinous processes; transverse spinous processes cannot be felt; vetebrae feel rounded; spinous processes, ribs, tailhead, tuber coxae and ischii prominent; withers, shoulders and neck structures are faintly discernible.

3. **Thin**   Fat buildup about halfway on spinous process; transverse spinous process cannot be felt; slight fat cover over ribs; spinous processes easily felt; tailhead prominent but individual vertebrae cannot be identified visually; tuber coxae rounded but easily seen; tuber ischii not apparent; withers, neck and shoulder accentuated.

4. **Moderately thin**   Slight ridge along back; faint outline of ribs discernible; tailhead prominence depends on conformation, fat can be felt around it; tuber coxae not discernible; withers, shoulders and neck not obviously thin.

5. **Moderate**   Back is flat (no crease or ridge); ribs not visually distinguishable but easily felt; fat around tailhead beginning to feel spongy; withers appear rounded over spinous processes; shoulders and neck blend smoothly into body.

6. **Moderately fleshy**   May have slight crease down back; fat over ribs is spongy; fat around tailhead soft; fat beginning to be deposited along the side of withers, behind shoulders and along neck.

7. **Fleshy**   May have crease down back; individual ribs can be felt but noticeable filling between ribs with fat; fat around tailhead soft; fat deposited along withers, behind shoulders and along neck.

8. **Fat**   Crease down back; difficult to feel ribs; fat around tailhead very soft; area along withers filled with fat; areas behind shoulders filled with fat; noticeable thickening of neck; fat deposited along inner thighs.

9. **Extremely fat**   Obvious crease down back; patchy fat over ribs; bulging fat around tailhead, along withers, behind shoulders and along neck; fat along inner thighs may rub together; flank filled with fat.

Once you are satisfied with your horse's condition, keep track of its weight to make sure that you are feeding your horse the appropriate amount of feed. Weight changes don't happen quickly in horses. By keeping track of your horse's weight, you'll go a long way toward avoiding some feed-related problems.

Fat Horses

If your horse is too fat, it's your fault. After all, horses love to eat, and they can only eat what you feed them or allow them to eat. The fact that horses eat for as much as seventeen hours in a twenty-four-hour period in the wild is irrelevant because these horses tend to eat low-calorie grasses and walk around all day, as opposed to their overweight cousins who sit in stalls all day eating higher-calorie feeds and buckets of horse treats. Horses kept in stalls can't get enough exercise to keep from getting fat if they are fed too much.

Fat isn't healthy on a horse. Fat horses can't tolerate exercise as well as horses in good condition. Fat acts like a layer of insulation around the horse. Being so well insulated, the fat horse can't get rid of the body heat that's generated during exercise; thus, a fat horse can overheat and fail to perform well (or stop performing altogether). In addition, chronic obesity is definitely associated with laminitis (a serious inflammatory condition of the feet) and with the occurrence of fat tumors (lipomas) in the abdomen. (Lipomas can twist around the intestine and result in your horse going to the hospital for colic surgery.)

Don't let your horse get fat. If he does, reduce his feed or increase his exercise (or both). Minimize or eliminate any grain. Alternatively, if you're concerned that your horse will get bored with so little to eat, you can switch to the same amount of a lower-calorie feed (say from alfalfa hay to grass or cereal grain hay).

Thin Horses

A thin horse, on the other hand, can be a much more involved diagnostic challenge than a fat horse, although most of the time it isn't. Any number of things can result in a horse being too thin, but as a practical matter, the most common cause of thinness has something to do with the feed. Generally, horses are too thin because the feed is of such poor quality that it can't possibly fill their nutritional needs or because the amount of feed that the horses are getting isn't enough to satisfy their energy requirements.

For example, say that you have four horses in a pasture together. Three of them look great; one of them is too thin. Oh sure, that thin horse may have a problem with its teeth or its liver or with internal parasites. But it's far more likely that the thin horse is the low man on the totem pole and is getting chased off its feed by its fat friends. While it certainly makes sense to investigate other problems that could be causing the horse in this example to lose weight, you certainly don't want to overlook the most obvious and common cause: The horse isn't getting enough to eat.

In stabled situations, if your horse is too thin, you will assume that your horse is getting enough feed. However, since you don't give out the food yourself, you really don't know how much feed your horse is getting, even if you ask for extra feed (this is not to impugn anyone's credibility, but you do have to investigate all possibilities).

If your horse exercises a lot, it may have trouble keeping up its weight. Exercise takes calories; calories come in the feed; if there's not enough feed, the horse will draw on the energy stored as fat in its body to supply the needs. Heavily exercising horses may need as much as 100 percent more energy than that required just to maintain their weight!

If your horse is thin because you're asking it to use a lot of calories, you have to give it calories in the diet. You may not be able to do this by just feeding hay. That's because, as big an animal as a horse is, its stomach is relatively small. A horse can fill up its stomach on forages before it's able to get enough calories to supply its needs. Thus, skinny horses that exercise a lot generally need to be fed extra calories in small, concentrated packages such as fortified grains and fats.

It's also possible that you have a horse that doesn't put on weight easily. There are metabolic differences between individual horses. For horses that don't keep their weight easily, the only solution is to give them more feed than you think they need. Feeding these horses more calories in a smaller package, such as is available in fats and grains, will help put and keep weight on horses that tend to be thin.

Finally, realize that it takes time for a horse to gain weight. If you want your adult horse to put on half a pound a day (a pretty good rate of gain), it will take 100 days to put on 50 pounds. It can take months to get an underweight horse up to where you want him. If you need some sort of reassurance that your horse is putting on weight, use the weight tape or the combination of girth and body length measurements to keep track of it. These tools will help you measure the gains (and hopefully help you build patience).

FEEDING OLDER HORSES

Trying to decide when a horse is old is like trying to decide when someone is bald. Everybody can recognize a bald head, but it's kind of hard to tell when hair loss first begins. As successive hairs are lost, you can see that the person is going bald but also that he or she still has a good amount of hair. Finally, once the person has lost enough hair, everyone will agree that he or she is bald. But trying to define that exact point when a person goes from thinning to bald is pretty much impossible.

It's pretty much the same way as horses age. If you use the definition provided by the American Quarter Horse Association, any horse older than sixteen is "aged." Don't tell the horse that; many horses remain useful and even competitive well into their twenties. Still, many older horses, however you define "older," do require some special attention (nutritional and otherwise).

A common complaint in otherwise healthy older horses is the failure to keep or gain weight. To some extent, this may be a reflection of the aging process; horses over twenty have been shown to be less able to digest fiber, protein and phosphorus than are younger horses (nobody is sure why). This implies that, to maintain their weight, some older horses may need to receive a bit more feed than younger horses of the same weight. In fact, the nutrient requirements of older horses are more like those of a yearling than they are like those of mature horses.

As a practical matter, you should take a few things into consideration if you are feeding an older horse. The diet should probably have elevated levels of protein (above 12 percent) and phosphorus (a minimum of 0.35 percent). Since older horses don't digest fiber well, you should avoid giving them forages that are extremely mature at the time they are harvested. Use good-quality green forages instead. Adding yeast cultures to the diet may also help with fiber digestion.

But beyond that, older horses may have particular problems that require special attention. You certainly want to check to make sure that your older horse is in good general health. Older horses are more prone to a variety of medical problems such as tumors of the pituitary gland and disease of the kidneys and liver. If your older horse isn't keeping its weight up, you certainly want it to have a thorough checkup with your veterinarian to make sure there's not some illness going on rather than just assuming that you need to toss in more feed.

You're also undoubtedly aware that horses require regular dental care. Smoothing sharp edges and leveling the chewing surfaces (called "floating" the teeth) is part of a regular health care program that should be provided by your horse's veterinarian. Certainly, you should make sure that your older horse has his teeth looked after. However, older horses have particular dental problems that aren't shared by their younger cohorts.

Older horses also *lose* their teeth as they age. A five-year-old horse has a tooth root that's several inches long; over the life of the horse, the root is continually exposed. The tooth root gets shorter as tooth continually grinds against tooth over the chewing life of the horse. Eventually, the entire tooth is worn down and it falls out. (Interestingly, one of the reasons old elephants die is that they lose their teeth.) You can't really do anything once a horse has lost a tooth, but it's still important to take care of the teeth that are left. However, a horse without all its teeth can't chew its feed normally. You'll often see old horses that are missing teeth drop partially chewed wads of hay out of their mouth ("quidding" the feed).

To compensate for the loss of teeth, you may need to feed your older horse hay that's already been ground up. Hay cubes, hay pellets or chaff are usually well accepted by older horses, and they're easy to store and measure. If your older horse can't even handle hay that's been chopped up, you can make a soup by soaking the cubes or pellets in water. Although it's a bit of a pain to prepare, most horses do just fine on this type of diet. If your horse needs more calories than can be provided by just feeding hay, adding grains or fats to the diet can help. There are also numerous feed products that combine hays and grains and are wonderfully suited for the nutritional needs of older horses. (There's really nothing special about "senior" feeds from a nutritional standpoint; they just have different amounts of all the same stuff that's found in any feed.)

CHAPTER 8

Feeding for Growth and Reproduction

ONCE PEOPLE START OWNING HORSES, THEY SEEM TO want to have more of them. Thus, horse owners enter the world of breeding horses and then raising the young ones. Like every other horse, these horses must be fed to maintain their normal body functions, but they also have special nutritional requirements that must be met.

FEEDING FOR OPTIMUM REPRODUCTION

Feeding Your Stallion

Stallions don't have any special nutrient requirements, but depending on how many mares they are supposed to breed or if they tend to fret and loose weight, they may need some extra energy in their diet. Breeding stallions may have energy requirements that are as much as 25 percent above what is needed for maintenance. Stallions don't need extra vitamins beyond their normal requirements; some people believe that breeding stallions need extra vitamin A (they don't) or that extra vitamin E increases sexual drive or improves the semen (it doesn't). Like all horses, breeding stallions should be fed diets made up primarily of high-quality forage, but the extra energy that's needed can be supplied in the form of a vitamin- and mineral-fortified processed grain concentrate, with the possible addition of some fat for extra calories, if necessary.

Feeding Your Broodmare

If you want to get your mare pregnant, one of the best things you can do for her is to keep her in good condition, even with a little bit of fat on her (between 5 and 7 on the Condition Score list; see page 86). Research has shown that compared to thin mares, mares that are in good body condition:

- Begin their reproductive cycle earlier in the year.
- Require fewer breeding cycles to get pregnant.
- Have a higher rate of pregnancy.
- Are more likely to keep their pregnancies (and not abort their fetuses).

If your mare is too thin, you can help her reproductive performance by putting some weight on her. You have to be a bit careful, of course; you don't want to just start dumping grain to a thin mare (as previously noted, that brings its own set of problems). Adding fat to the ration of a thin brood mare is a good option. Proper management of the brood mare's body condition is very important in supporting conception and in promoting normal foal growth.

Feeding Your Pregnant Mare

This probably comes as something of a surprise to you, but the fact is that you don't have to do anything extra for your pregnant mare for the first eight months of her pregnancy. Just feed her like a normal adult horse, with the proper amounts of good-quality feed. The baby inside your mare doesn't need any special attention.

However, as the mare enters her last three months of gestation, her nutrient requirements began to increase because the baby starts to grow more rapidly (about a pound a day!). The requirements for energy, protein, calcium, phosphorus and vitamin A all go up, too. Energy requirements are estimated to go up by 11, 13 and 20 percent during the ninth, tenth and eleventh months of gestation, respectively. Trying to get energy into your pregnant mare is further complicated by the fact that as pregnancy proceeds, the mare's stomach may get squeezed by the growing baby, decreasing the mare's desire and ability to eat.

Thus, even when you've got good hay or pasture to feed your brood mare, adding some vitamin- and mineral-fortified processed grain concentrate that's between 14 and 18 percent protein will help provide her with the extra things she needs to develop a healthy foal. Fortified grain concentrates can be fed at levels of between 0.5 and 1.0 percent of body weight (that's as much as 10 pounds in a 1000-pound horse). Of course, mares that are maintaining a normal body condition during their pregnancy will be on the low end of the scale and fat mares should be fed little if any grain (although they still need supplemental vitamins or minerals).

Feeding Your Lactating Mare

Making milk requires a lot of extra energy from the mare. This means that she will need a lot of extra feed, especially in the first couple of months, when the baby seems to be hanging onto her udder all the time (and probably is). A mare in early lactation may eat up to 3 percent of her body weight per day in feed (which is double what she might need just to maintain her own body weight).

· FIGURE 5 ·

You'll most likely have to supplement your lactating mare with a vitamin- and mineral-fortified processed grain concentrate to keep her from losing weight. Her protein requirements will go up a little bit, too, so the grain ration should probably have some extra protein in it. A sample diet for a lactating mare might consist of free-choice hay and a fortified grain concentrate fed at a rate of 0.5 to 1.5 percent of the mare's body weight.

This weight thing is important. If your mare is thin or losing weight during lactation, it may be hard to get her back in foal. On the other hand, if she's fat, lactation is a good time to allow the mare to use her fat reserves to produce milk (and regain her svelte, girlish figure).

It's interesting to note that what you feed the mare really doesn't seem to affect the composition of the milk. There haven't been many studies on this, but it appears that lactating mares fed hay and grain produce milk of the same nutritional caliber as do lactating mares that are fed just hay. As long as you realize that your mare is going to need extra nutrition when she makes milk, she will continue to make milk. But you can't make her produce "better" milk by the way you feed her.

FEEDING GROWING HORSES

There's probably more discussion about the "best" way to feed a young horse than there is for horses of any other age. In reality, young horses are no different from any other horse, in that they have certain nutritional requirements and those requirements can be met by any number of feed combinations. Still, there's often more to raising a young horse than just making sure that it's healthy. That's because the people who start off with young horses generally do so because they want to sell them; when it comes to the value of a young horse, bigger is often perceived as better (and bigger usually means a higher price). Unfortunately, it seems as though the bigger you try to get a young horse to grow and the faster you try to get it there, the more likely you are to run into problems.

Horses grow fastest early in life. By the time they're eighteen months old, they've reached about 80 percent of their expected mature weight and about 94 percent of their mature height. What this means is that anything you are going to do to and for your young horse has to be started early to have any effect. The goal in feeding young horses is to feed them so they can grow, but not to put too much stress on their system. To keep track of this, you should try to keep some sort of records as to how your horse is growing in order to prevent any surprises (such as, "Oh my gosh, he wasn't fat yesterday!"). Remember, most horses are supposed to grow up to be athletes, and fat athletes, aren't that common (especially fat runners).

The most important nutritional factors to consider in growing horses are energy, protein, calcium and phosphorus. Sure, things like vitamins and other minerals are important, too, but you have to make sure that the big things are right before you start worrying about little things like the amount of trace minerals in the diet. Here are some general things to consider about each of these components:

- **Energy**   As young horses get bigger, they need more energy. Even though the growth rate of young horses slows down (and requires less energy), as they get bigger, their need for energy to maintain body functions increases. One easy way to make sure that a young, growing horse has enough energy in its diet is to allow free access to hay.

- **Protein**   As a percentage of their body weight, young horses have a higher protein requirement than do older horses. This is due to two facts: Young horses need additional protein in their diet for their growing body tissues, and the amount of feed they eat is

100

small and must be packed with protein to meet the requirements. Research studies have also shown that a greater amount of the essential amino acid lysine is needed by the young horse for growth than is available from bacteria in its intestinal tract or from many feeds. For this reason, high-quality protein sources need to be fed to young horses. A high-quality protein source is one that contains a high proportion of essential amino acids. Alfalfa, soybean meal, canola meal and milk protein products are good choices to supply the additional lysine required in the diets of young horses.

- **Minerals**   Contrary to popular belief, most horses are quite forgiving when it comes to the "ideal" level of minerals in their diets. The range between too much and not enough is pretty big. In fact, there's probably more *not* known today about mineral levels and interactions than *is* known, and it's hard to come up with (or support) a lot of rigid recommendations. However, the most important minerals to consider in growing horses are calcium and phosphorus, which are needed for normal bone growth and development. About the only thing you can say for sure is that the level of calcium in the diet should exceed the level of phosphorus; a calcium:phosporus balance of anywhere from 1.1:1 to 6:1 seems to be just fine for young horses, as long as both calcium and phosphorus requirements are met. Again, feeding legume hays, which tend to have high amounts of calcium in them, will help ensure an adequate calcium level in young horses.

Far more attention is paid to levels of vitamins in young horses than is probably necessary. This may be due in part to the fact that people are bombarded (in many cases, unnecessarily) about the need for vitamins in their own lives as well as in the lives of their horses. In fact, a young horse that is supplied with good-quality hay and provided a vitamin-fortified grain mix should be able to easily meet all its vitamin requirements without needing any extra supplementation.

A real hot topic in young horse nutrition research involves trace minerals. Previously ignored trace minerals such as copper, zinc and manganese, have all been given research attention recently. While certain trace minerals may play a role in normal growth and development, wholesale supplementation is not necessarily the way to solve any problems. You should consult with veterinarians and/or equine nutritionists in your area to see whether there are any specific trace mineral concerns that need to be addressed when you put together a diet for your growing horse.

Of course, proper feeding is not the only factor that you have to think about when you're considering how your baby horse grows. There are genetic factors at work (you are not going to get your pony foal to grow to seventeen hands, no matter what you feed it). Diseases and internal parasites can also affect the growth rate of babies. Your influence on your baby horse's growth is limited to the nutrition you provide; in this area, you should at least try do the best you possibly can.

Feeding Babies

One of the nice things about feeding baby horses is that they come with their own feed supply. Mare's milk is an ideal source of nutrients for young horses, and virtually every mare does a pretty good job of supplying her foal with all the nutrients it needs for the first sixty to ninety days of its life. During that time, the foal will also begin to nose around and eat Mom's feed, providing all sorts of great and endearing photo opportunities. (The babies will also eat the mare's manure, which, while less endearing, is also perfectly harmless. In fact, some people assert that eating the mare's manure is *necessary* to populate the growing baby's intestinal tract with bacteria.)

At two or three months of age, you should consider creep feeding your baby. Creep feeding is done largely to provide extra energy and minerals that are needed for optimum growth. *Creep feeders* are ingenious devices with slots in them large enough to allow the baby's nose in but small enough to keep out the mare. You should creep feed your baby a 16 percent protein, vitamin-fortified grain mix, putting feed that is about 1.0 to 1.5 percent of the baby's body weight per day in the creep feeder. Other ways to think about the proper amount of creep feed are 0.5 to 1.0 pound of feed per hundred pounds of baby or about one pound of feed per month of age (up to approximately six or seven months of age).

Creep feeding has a bit of an undeserved bad reputation because some people have creep fed unlimited amounts of feed to their babies and have ended up with developmental problems. You certainly don't want to overfeed baby horses. However, like many things (cars, guns and so on), the problem isn't the device itself; it's how you use it.

Feeding Weanlings

Weaning a baby horse from its mom is a time of serious stress for mare, foal and owner. There's no "best" time to wean a foal; they can be successfully weaned as early as two months of age. No matter when you wean them, however, expect some sort of short-term decrease in performance due to the stress. Of course, you'd like to minimize the stress of weaning as much as possible, and if you've creep fed your baby, there shouldn't be much interruption to its growth rate.

There's a lot of concern—possibly too much—among horse owners about making weanlings grow too fast. Much of that concern centers on carbohydrate intake. While high levels of carbohydrate intake have been associated with developmental orthopedic problems in some horses, other studies have failed to show orthopedic problems in rapidly growing weanlings. It's generally recommended that extremely fast growth rates or growth spurts (caused by inconsistent levels of nutrition) be avoided in wean-lings, but the problems of developmental orthopedic disease are much more complicated than just feeding too much energy.

Of course, since people worry so much about their weanlings grow-ing too rapidly, sometimes they overreact and end up starving them. If, in trying to prevent developmental orthopedic problems, you severely restrict either the amount of energy or the amount of protein that a weanling horse gets, you can very effectively limit its growth and end up with a much smaller horse than you had hoped for. Although you don't want a horse with developmental orthopedic problems, you don't want one that is rough-coated and stunted, either. The bottom line is that a well-balanced diet for growth should not contribute to orthopedic abnormalities.

Weanlings should eat from 1 to 1.5 percent of their body weight per day in a 14.5 to 16 percent protein, vitamin-fortified grain concentrate, as well as all the good-quality forage they can eat. This means that many weanlings can eat as much as six to nine pounds of grain concentrate per day (but no more than 60 percent of the weanling's ration should be in the form of grain). With better-quality forage (for example, high-quality alfalfa hay), many young horses don't need much grain to supply extra energy. However, the grain they do get must be well fortified to provide essential nutrients that may be lacking in the hay.

Feeding Yearlings

By the time your young horse is a year old, its growth rate will have started to slow down. As horses get bigger, the concentration of nutri-ents in the diet can decrease (especially protein), in part because they can eat more.

Yearlings should eat from 1 to 1.25 percent of their body weight per day in a 13 to 14 percent protein, vitamin-fortified grain concentrate, plus all the good-quality forage they can eat. This means that many yearlings can eat from 8 to 12 pounds (about 3.5 to 5.5 kilos) of grain concentrate per day, but the ratio of hay to grain should be no more than 1:1.

At first glance, you may think, "No one in their right mind would ever feed a yearling 8 to 12 pounds of grain." Although this may seem like a lot, it's really not. Commercial vitamin- and mineral-fortified grain supplements for yearlings are designed to provide not only adequate energy for growth but also the proper levels of vitamins and minerals. If you don't feed your yearling according to the manufacturer's recommendations, your yearling's diet may not be adequately fortified. If you've got any questions about a particular product, ask your veterinarian or a nutritionist for some help and advice (it's always better to be safe than sorry).

CHAPTER 9

Feeding Performance Horses

IF YOU OWN A HORSE THAT IS USED FOR PERFORMANCE, you are going to have to feed it. Presumably, you are also going to want the horse (and yourself) to do the very best you can during the competition. That means that you are going to spend endless hours working with your horse in training for the big event (whatever event that might be). Of course, in the course of all this preparation, you can't forget to feed your horse.

Performance events make unique demands on the horse's system. From a nutritional standpoint, performance mostly increases the energy your horse will use. Your performance horse will have to be given more energy in order to perform; more energy equates to more feed.

Providing energy to your performance horse is not just a matter of tossing it a few extra flakes of hay, however. There have been dozens of studies evaluating different ways to feed horses that exercise. Once you understand the principles, feeding these horses becomes relatively simple. But there are a couple of other important considerations when it comes to feeding performance horses.

When to Feed

For a long time, it was felt that the most important thing that helped an equine athlete perform was the blood sugar level. Thus, many horses that exercised were given meals a few hours before exercise began, in an effort to raise their blood sugar (and presumably their energy) level. Unfortunately, this doesn't appear to work.

If you feed a horse the grain portion of its diet less than three hours before the onset of exercise you can hormonally put the horse at a disadvantage. After you feed grain, there is a surge in blood glucose as the starches in the grain are being digested. The blood sugar surge also results in a surge in insulin, the hormone produced by the horse's pancreas, whose duty it is to put the excess blood glucose into storage. This process takes some time because starch digestion and the increases in blood glucose and insulin that follow usually last from four to six hours. If a horse begins exercise during the period that blood insulin is high, the horse will be trying to put glucose in storage instead of releasing the glucose to be used for energy. As exercise continues, you will see a crash of blood glucose levels below those seen in even the resting horse.

As far as providing energy for the horse, what's important is not the level of sugar that's absorbed into the horse's blood. Rather, it's the ability of the horse to use the energy that's already stored in its body (as fat and as a carbohydrate store known as *glycogen*). Thus, you want to have the circulating insulin levels relatively low in an exercising horse. If a horse is fed grain eight hours or more before exercise, the glucose and insulin peaks will be back to resting levels. Then, when exercise starts, the release of glucose for energy from the energy storage areas can proceed more efficiently.

Interestingly, feeding hay or grass has very little effect on glucose and insulin because there is not that much starch in plants. Similarly, feeding fat to horses helps keep the blood glucose levels down and may help promote a more efficient release of glucose into the blood when it's needed. In fact, diets that are high in fiber and fat offer a lot of advantages for many exercising horses.

WHAT TO FEED

What you feed your performance horse depends largely on what you want to do with the horse. As you know, the foundation of the diet has to be forage; if additional calories are needed, they can be provided in the form of fats or carbohydrates. There's been a lot of work done fairly recently examining the benefits of feeding significant amounts of fat to horses.

Adding fat to a horse's diet increases the amount of energy without substantially increasing the volume of feed that the horse has to eat. Research has shown that providing fat can offer some terrific advantages for the diet of certain horses. Fats are very efficient energy sources because they tend to produce lower internal temperatures in the horse when they are digested than grains produce; the inability to get rid of the body heat that's produced during exercise is one of the things that limits a horse's ability to perform. Adding fat to the diet also tends to decrease the amount of feed a horse eats; that means there will tend to be less weight in the intestine of a horse that's fed a significant amount of fat (up to 10 percent of the diet). Another potential benefit of feeding fat to a horse is that it accustoms the body to using the fat that's stored in the body as an energy source during work. Since the fat stores in the horse's body are a lot larger than the stores of glycogen in the muscle, if a horse can use stored fat for energy, it can potentially work for a much longer time than if it has to run off of the stored muscle sugar.

Research has also shown that adding fat to a horse's diet can help maintain normal blood sugar levels. After grain meals (with lots of carbohydrates), blood sugar levels have been shown to rise rapidly; the rise in blood sugar after a meal with fat in it is much less profound. Some people have suggested that a rise in blood sugar is associated with horses getting overly energetic or "high." Thus, there may be some advantage to feeding fat to horses in which calmness is desired, such as show hunters or western pleasure horses. In fact, it's pretty hard to find fault with adding fat to the diet of *any* performance horse.

To a large extent, what you feed your performance horse should be dictated by the type of exercise it does. To that end, exercise performance can be divided into the three categories discussed next.

High-Intensity, Short-Duration Exercise (Flat Track Horses, Polo Horses, Barrel Racers)

During this type of exercise, the horse is working as hard as it can, as fast as the heart can beat. A horse can keep up this level of performance for a short time only (less than ten minutes). Horses that work under these conditions exercise anaerobically (the cells are working so hard that they have to produce energy without the benefit of adequate oxygen; the body can't supply blood to the tissues fast enough to keep up with the demand for oxygen). Horses that work anaerobically have to use the energy that's stored in their muscles.

You don't want to feed these horses grain within four hours of exercise because of the effect of insulin. You don't want to feed them large amounts of hay prior to exercise, either, because this increases the amount of weight (from feed and water) they have to tote around. On the other hand, since it takes feed twenty-four to forty-eight hours to go from the mouth to the anus, there's unlikely to be any significant benefit from a short-term fast for horses that work hard for a short period of time because there's already feed in the horse.

Fasting a horse for twelve hours is not practical for everyday training, however. In fact, you might even argue that training a horse with extra weight in its gut might help out on the day of competition, for the same reason baseball players swing weighted bats while waiting for their turn to hit. The bat feels lighter and easier to swing when the weight is removed. In the same manner, by fasting for twelve hours prior to competition a horse that participates in short-duration, high-intensity exercise may gain a slight weight advantage.

Bottom line? Don't give these horses any hay for twelve hours prior to competitive exercise to decrease the amount of weight they have to carry. Don't feed any grain within eight hours of exercise. Let them drink all the water they want. Then, run them as fast as they can.

Moderate-Intensity, Medium-Duration Exercise (Show Horses)

This type of exercise is typical of horses that have to perform in a number of classes during the day. Speed usually isn't the main concern with these horses; thus, the weight of feed they have to carry around in their gut isn't a big concern. Endurance is also not that big an issue; in fact, many horse trainers don't want their show horses to be too fit, lest they be too energetic. Show horses would probably benefit from small, frequent forage meals, both to help relieve the tedium of standing around between classes and to help stay hydrated. However, as with all performance horses, you should probably avoid a grain meal within eight hours of exercise because of the insulin effect.

Bottom line? Feed show horses small, frequent forage meals. Don't give grain within eight hours of exercise (to avoid any unwanted insulin effects). Let them drink all the water they want. Then, don't knock over any rails or keep going forward (as the case may be).

· FIGURE 6 ·

Low-Intensity, Long-Duration Exercise (Endurance Horses)

Endurance riding is mostly aerobic work. Thus, the major sources of energy for these horses come from the production of volatile fatty acids from the digestion of fiber and from the stores of body fat. In the endurance horse it is really important to keep the gut full of fiber so there can be continuous energy production. Endurance horses also sweat a lot and can lose significant amounts of water and electrolytes; fiber in the gut also holds water and electrolytes that can be drawn on during exercise when necessary. Thus, feeding good-quality hay (or pasture) is the basis of a good endurance-horse diet. Quality is the key word here. Good-quality hay is more digestible; thus, more of it can be used for energy.

Training increases the ability of the horse to mobilize and utilize fat stores for energy. There is some thought that by adding fat to the diet, the body becomes more adept at mobilizing it for utilization. Because of this theory and the fact that fat is very *energy dense* (you can feed less of it and get more energy), high-fat diets have become very popular with endurance riders.

Bottom line? Feed grain and/or fat the night before a competition (unless you are in Australia, where they start at midnight) and free-choice hay until the beginning of the competition. Give electrolytes before the ride and early during the ride (prior to significant dehydration) as this has been shown to help delay the onset of fatigue. Let your endurance horse drink all the water it wants. Then, ride as fast and as smart as you can (and make sure your horse's pulse and respiration rates are at a decent level before you bother entering the veterinary stop).

CHAPTER 10

Feeding Horses with Disease Conditions

Proper nutrition is important in the management, treatment and even the cause of a variety of disease conditions in the horse. While proper nutrition certainly isn't the answer to everything that afflicts the horse, in many cases it certainly can help!

COLIC PREVENTION

The word *colic* is one of the oldest terms in medicine, dating from Classical times. The word doesn't refer to a specific disease; it merely refers to pain that originates from the horse's abdomen. Colic is obviously an important conditionh of the horse. It's been estimated that up to 50 percent of all medical problems in the horse relate to the horse's abdomen; many of those problems cause signs of colic.

Diet is frequently fingered as the cause for most cases of colic. It sort of makes sense; it's not much of a stretch to conclude that what you put into the horse's digestive tract might have something to do with the problems that occur there. Yet there's really not much scientific evidence that diet or specific nutrients are the cause of most cases of colic in the horse.

Still, some specific dietary risk factors for colic have been identified. What's particularly interesting about all these factors is that you can do something about them. (That's a nice distinction from a lot of things that have to do with horses and their health.) These factors include:

- Sudden feed changes. Three studies have shown that recent changes in the diet increased the risk of colic. One of the studies showed that colic was most likely to occur within two weeks of the feed change; another showed that two or more changes in hay or one or more change in grain concentrate during a year increased the chance that a horse would colic. This suggests that if a horse owner makes multiple changes in a horse's diet, the risk for colic will increase.

- Irregular feeding schedules. Horses should be fed on a regular schedule so as to keep feed in their intestine. Feeding several times a day offers a number of theoretical advantages for horses and more closely mimics their natural behavior, but an "optimal" feeding schedule for the horse has yet to be determined.

- Spoiled or moldy feed. Why in the world would you want to give spoiled feed to your horse, anyway?

- Decreased water intake, which may lead to impaction-type colics (an *impaction* is a plug in the tube that is the intestine; constipation is one kind of impaction). Decreased water consumption can be a particular problem in cold weather. It's been shown that horses will drink more water if it's kept between 45 and 75 degrees Fahrenheit. Thus, water heaters may be more than a nice convenience when the weather turns cold.

- Feeding too soon after exercise. Exercise normally causes a decrease in the movement of the intestines. It's reasonable to think that a change in intestinal movement could be associated with some cases of colic. Cool your horse thoroughly before feeding it.

- Well-fed horses that are stalled for most of the day. Regular exercise appears to be an important factor in helping to decrease the incidence of colic.

- Overeating or eating too rapidly. This can be a particular problem if horses are fed cubed or pelleted rations. This is another reason why it may be beneficial to feed your horse several times a day.
- Feeding large amounts of grain concentrates. Two studies have suggested that the more grain a horse eats, the more likely it will be to colic. It's been well demonstrated that feeding large amounts of grain to a horse causes changes in the horse's hindgut. Eating concentrates increases the production of lactic acid, which makes the contents of the hindgut more acidic and results in water movement in and out of the bowel. Hypothetically, this can cause some horses to develop distention of various parts of the hindgut with gas and/or fluid, inflammation of the intestines themselves or the formation of impactions. These changes may even be responsible for more serious colics, such as displacements or *torsions* (twisting) of the colon.
- Processed feeds. The more these feeds are processed, such as pellets or sweet feeds, the more the odds of a horse colicking, while diets made up of combinations of different feeds or whole grains did not significantly increase the odds of colic, when horses in both groups were compared to horses on forage only.
- Broodmares kept on lush grass and fed lots of grain to help keep them lactating. The grain is usually fed at night when the broodmares are brought into the barn. Increasing the turn-out time, providing hay in the pasture and keeping the grass in the pasture long (as opposed to mowing the pasture) are all management techniques that may have some benefit for the prevention of colic in broodmares.
- Feeding coarse, poor-quality hay (which can lead to impactions). Poor-quality forage is not well digested by the horse. As bad hay passes through the intestine, its stems are not broken down. Potentially, these stems can accumulate and plug up the tube.

There are some other things related to nutrition that you can do to help your horse avoid colic. Horses that are kept in sandy conditions (such as those in Arizona, California, and in parts of Nebraska and Florida) may tend to eat a lot of sand along with their feed; these horses should be fed off the ground and monitored for sand in their manure (and treated accordingly). Cantharidin toxicosis—caused by the blister beetle that's ordinarily found in the southern Great Plains states of the United States, but that has also been reported as far north as Minnesota—is a serious problem caused by ingestion of alfalfa hay in which the beetles have been crushed (it takes as few as two to five beetles to cause colic); make sure that you buy your hay from known, reputable growers. Monensin and solumycin, additives in poultry and cattle feed, can cause colic (or worse); you should only feed your horse feeds designed for horses.

COLIC TREATMENT

If, in spite of your best efforts to prevent it, your horse has had an episode of colic, nutritional management can be important in treatment, too. Here are some specific situations in which nutrition is involved in the management of post-colic cases:

- After impactions. Horses with impactions shouldn't be fed until the obstruction of the intestine has been taken care of. You don't want to go packing more feed behind an already existing plug in the gut. The best evidence that the impaction has resolved is the regular passage of manure (although it can also be confirmed by a rectal examination performed by your veterinarian).
- After surgery. Of course, in most instances the reintroduction of feed following colic surgery is going to be the responsibility of the hospital at which your horse is residing. One big problem that can

occur after colic surgery is that the intestine may be reluctant to start moving again. Usually, small amounts of water are initially offered to the post-surgical horse, followed by increasing amounts of hay or wet forage mashes as normal gut function returns.

- After impactions of the cecum. The horse's cecum is part of the hindgut that's analogous to a person's appendix. It's an approximately three-foot thumb off the main pipe. In some horses, the cecum can become impacted with feed (and it can be a real pain to get the feed out of there). After the cecum has been emptied (either medically or after surgery), it will often fill right back up with feed; the stretching and dilation caused by the impaction apparently messes up the normal movement of the cecum. Thus, small amounts of feeds that are low in bulk (such as pellets) are generally given to these horses for a while after the problem resolves (and even then some horses reimpact).

- After removal of a significant portion of the small intestine. In some types of colic, small intestine has to be removed, usually because of injury caused by a lack of blood supply. (In some types of colic, it's as if someone had put a rubber band around part of the intestine.) If more than 60 percent of the small intestine is removed, horses can experience chronic weight loss and a loss of appetite. Careful management can help many of these horses. Horses that have had significant portions of their small intestines removed should be fed things that are absorbed by the large intestines, such as easily fermentable, good-quality roughage. Grain concentrates should be avoided, since they are normally processed in the small intestine and can cause problems if too much gets to the hindgut. These horses may also benefit from the addition to their diet of such things as beet pulp, wheat or rice bran, or fats (such as vegetable oil).

- After removal of a significant portion of the large intestine. Large intestine has to be removed from some colicking horses for reasons similar to those that necessitate removal of the small intestine. Horses who have had the majority of their large colon removed should be fed diets relatively high in energy, protein and phosphorus, such as can be provided with alfalfa hay and grain.
- After small colon problems. Diseases of the last portion of the hindgut, the small colon, can cause problems if feed is reintroduced to the affected horse too soon. Low bulk, complete feeds may be the best way to help keep the amount of material going through the intestine to a minimum in these horses.

The problem of colic in the horse is a complex one. Nutrition is not the only cause of, nor the only solution to the problem. For those of you interested in learning more about colic, there's a *Concise Guide to Colic in the Horse* to provide you with a wealth of additional information.

LAMINITIS

Laminitis is inflammation of the tissues that connect the sensitive structures of the hoof to the dead hoof that protects them. The connections between the tissues are very much like the connections between the covering paper and a popular chocolate-covered peanut butter cup. The connections are called the *laminae*; inflammation of these structures is called laminitis.

There are many causes of laminitis in the horse. Many well-recognized causes have dietary underpinnings. Among reported nutritional causes of laminitis are the following:

- Carbohydrate overload (occurring from large grain meals or when the horse breaks into the feed room).

- Lush green grass (perhaps related to insufficient fiber).
- Chronic obesity.
- Drinking lots of cold water if a horse isn't continuing to exercise. (Exercising horses should be allowed to drink all the water they want.)
- Eating black walnut shavings that are used for stall bedding.

The treatment of a horse with acute laminitis is a true veterinary emergency. You'll recognize it in most cases; affected horses walk stiffly and try to get weight off their front feet. The best way to treat laminitis is to manage your horse's diet well and to avoid it in the first place.

HYPP

Hyperkalemic periodic paralysis (HYPP) is a well-documented genetic disease of the American Quarter Horse that appears to have originated with the famous stallion Impressive. The disease involves the inability of cells in the body to regulate the concentrations of the two most important electrolytes, sodium and potassium. The disease can be detected by a blood test.

As a result of HYPP, the affected horse's muscles may be contracting almost all the time (even though you may not be able to see the contractions). Although this isn't really a problem in most cases, under certain circumstances (especially under stress), the abnormal muscle contraction can become a really big deal and result in things like:

- Waves of muscle twitching down the ribs and into the flank.
- The third eyelid coming up.
- Stiffness and muscle rigidity (as is seen when a horse ties up; see later in this chapter).
- In extreme conditions, paralysis and even death.

Treatment of HYPP is directed at keeping potassium levels in the normal range. Although there are drugs that can help (such as the diuretic acetazolamide), dietary management of potassium intake has been shown to be critical in managing HYPP. Thus, grass hays (such as timothy, coastal Bermuda grass or oat) are preferred over legume hays (such as alfalfa and lezpedeza). Grass hays tend to have about half the potassium of legume hays. Similarly, cereal grains such as corn, oats and barley are low in potassium and can make up a good portion of the diet of a horse with HYPP. (You have to watch feeding cereal grains prepared using molasses, soybean meal or dehydrated alfalfa; these have higher concentrations of potassium in them.) Beet pulp can also be a big help in the management of horses with HYPP, since it's fairly high in fiber and low in potassium. Of course, the only way to determine the level of potassium in your horse's feed is to measure it, but with proper management, horses with HYPP can usually lead normal lives.

LIVER DISEASE

The liver is an organ that's essential for normal digestive function. When the liver gets sick (for whatever reason), the horse loses the ability to efficiently digest its feed. The object of feeding a horse with a sick liver is to try to make things as easy on the liver as possible.

Lower protein diets require less metabolic work from the liver than do higher protein diets; thus, grass hays are preferable to legume hays. In addition, the protein that is supplied should be high in a particular type of amino acid, called "branched chain" amino acids (a reference to their chemical structure). These amino acids are found in high quantities in sugar beet pulp and corn. Finally, many horses with liver disease are given supplemental B vitamins, since the metabolism of these vitamins takes place largely in the liver.

KIDNEY DISEASE

Horses with disease of the kidneys are helped by lowering their intake of calcium, since the sick horses lose their ability to regulate the body's calcium as the disease progresses. Thus, alfalfa or other legume hays that have lots of calcium in them should be avoided in these horses. Some horses with kidney problems also have low protein levels (they lose the protein out of their diseased kidneys) and may benefit from additional protein in their diet from such sources as linseed or soybean meal. (It used to be believed that horses with kidney disease should get low protein diets, but further work has shown that lowering the dietary protein content in a horse with chronic kidney disease doesn't do much to slow down the progression of the disease.)

RESPIRATORY DISEASE

Feeding horses with respiratory problems is important, not so much from a nutritional standpoint as from a feed quality perspective. It's been well shown that dust aggravates conditions such as chronic obstructive pulmonary disease or tracheitis (inflammation of the windpipe). Horses that eat dusty or moldy feeds may cough more because the dust particles irritate the airways.

There are a number of ways to control feed dust. Most importantly, feed good-quality feed. If you feed hay, it can be soaked in water for a few minutes immediately prior to feeding to keep the dust down. Alternatively, hay cubes or pellets tend to be less dusty than does loose hay. In areas where it is available, moist haylage or silage is a good feed for horses with respiratory problems. By keeping the dust down, your horse (and you) will breathe easier.

EMN

Equine motor neuron disease (EMN) was recognized relatively recently (in the early 1980s). It's a disease of the nerve fibers that provide the stimulus for normal muscle activity in the muscles that maintain the horse's posture (the condition in horses is very similar to Lou Gehrig's disease in people). Horses with EMN tremble while standing, lose the ability to lock their stifle joints, and lose weight. Curiously, they generally look worse standing or walking than they do trotting or cantering.

It's pretty much been determined that the cause of EMN is a chronic lack of vitamin E in the diet. Apparently, if there's not enough vitamin E, the affected nerves deteriorate. Horses need at least one international unit of vitamin E per pound of body weight; that level is usually provided in good-quality legume hay or green pasture. Unfortunately, grain and concentrate mixes often supply little or no vitamin E as a result of processing or storage. In fact, virtually all the reported cases of EMN have been seen in horses that were stabled or in dirt paddocks, fed grass hay and/or lots of grain and lack access to green forage.

The signs of EMN occur only when about 30 percent of the nerve fibers are lost. (This fact does make you wonder how a horse with a loss of 20 percent of the nerve fibers would perform.) Thus, the best way to deal with EMN is to prevent it. If your horse fits the profile of a horse likely to develop EMN, providing access to green forage or giving supplemental vitamin E in its diet is certainly not a bad idea.

EPM

Equine protozoal myelitis (EPM) is a disease of the nervous system caused by a protozoan parasite called *Sarcocystis neurona*. The disease is characterized by a number of vague signs related to improper function of the nervous system; accurate diagnosis of the condition requires analysis of the fluid that is normally found in the spinal canal.

There are two aspects of EPM that relate to nutrition. First, it's been conclusively demonstrated that *S. neurona* gets into the horse's feed through contamination from feces of the opossum. This certainly implies that you should try to keep opossums out of your horse's feed. However, it's been shown that an amazingly large number of otherwise normal horses have been exposed to *S. neurona* (as many as 50 percent of the horses studied in three states, according to studies released in February 1997). It seems unlikely that contamination of individual bits of feed is responsible for every case of exposure; thus, some folks suggest that feed could get contaminated *before* it gets to the farm or stables, during the process of handling and storage. This has led some veterinarians to advise that horses should be fed feeds that have been heat treated, such as cubed or pelleted hays or steam-crimped grains (the heat would kill the protozoa).

The second nutritional aspect of EPM involves supplementing horses that are being treated for the disease. A combination of two drugs, pyrimethamine and sulfadiazine, is usually prescribed for treatment. Working together, these drugs mess up the use by the protozoa of folic acid (which is used to make DNA, the substance that has all the information the organism needs to reproduce itself). Horses need folic acid, too; fortunately, the folic acid in the protozoa is much more sensitive to the effects of the drugs than is that of the horse. Still, some horses treated for EPM occasionally show problems related to a deficiency in folic acid, particularly *anemia* (a lack of the red blood cells that carry oxygen throughout the horse's body). In some cases, adding supplemental folic acid to the diet of horses being treated for EPM may be considered. (For reasons too complicated to explain here, this aspect of EPM therapy is somewhat controversial; you should always consult your veterinarian before adding any supplement to your horse's ration if the horse is being treated for any disease.)

EXERTIONAL RHABDOMYOLYSIS (TYING UP)

Tying up is a rather annoying problem that afflicts some performance horses. Horses that tie up appear to be happily (although sometimes somewhat nervously) exercising along when all of a sudden their muscles lock up tighter than a drum. A horse that ties up goes rapidly from being free-moving poetry in motion to a more statuesque appearance.

The exact cause of tying up isn't known, although it's thought to be related to some defect that results in horses being unable to use the energy that's stored in their muscles as glycogen. In fact, there may be several underlying causes of the syndrome described as "tying up" (and that's at least one reason there's no single cure for every horse with the problem). While it's generally *not* a very serious condition, it certainly can be; in severe cases, imbalances in body fluids, kidney damage and even collapse can occur.

Which of the numerous available therapies employed in the treatment of horses that tie up is used in the treatment of a particular horse with the disease depends on the severity of the case and the person doing the treating. However, given that "an ounce of treatment is worth a pound of cure," there's a great deal of interest in trying to prevent the problem in the first place. Much of that interest is directed at nutrition.

The goal of dietary management of horses that tie up is to try to minimize or bypass the energy that's stored in the horse's muscles. This is done by trying to decrease the amount of carbohydrate in the diet and increasing the amount of fat. Thus, you basically eliminate grain from the diet of horses that tie up. Fat can be added in a couple of ways, either through the use of commercially available high-fat diets or by using oils (two cups of vegetable oil per day mixed with alfalfa pellets might be one place to start for a 1,000-pound horse). Additional nutritional avenues to travel with the horse that ties up include supplementation with vitamin E and selenium and possibly chromium. Combined with regular exercise (and a thorough warm-up at all gaits before beginning exercise), appropriate dietary management can go a long way toward helping to prevent this irritating condition.

EQUINE POLYSACCHARIDE STORAGE MYOPATHY

A distinct group of horses that show signs of tying up actually have a condition called *polysaccharide storage myopathy* (the only way to tell is by taking a small piece of muscle tissue and looking at it under a microscope). So far, the condition has been found only in quarter horses; a similar but more severe condition has also been seen in draught horses. Studies have suggested that affected horses can't use the energy stored in their muscles in a normal fashion. Management of these horses is similar to that for myositis, emphasizing good-quality hay, low amounts of grain, supplemental dietary fat and balanced levels of vitamins and minerals. Supplementation with additional vitamin E and selenium can also be considered.

FESCUE TOXICOSIS

Grazing on fescue grass that has been infected with a particular fungus (and its associated toxin) is associated with all sorts of reproductive problems in mares in late pregnancy, such as abortions, abnormal fetal position at birth, and placental problems and decreased milk production. There is also some evidence that nonpregnant mares that graze infected fescue grass pasture have decreased fertility rates. When you consider that fescue is the most common grass found in pastures in the United States and that the amount of it is increasing, the potential size of the problem is pretty sobering. So what do you do?

If you want, you can analyze your pasture to see if it's infected. This should be done in the fall, before the breeding season. If it is infected, you've got several options:

1. You can rip out your pasture and replant it with fungus-free fescue (and expensive and time-consuming option). One other problem with this option is that the fungus is actually good for the fescue; fungus-free fescue is actually less hardy than that which is infected.

2. You can manage the pasture so as to prevent the grass from flowering. The seed of the fescue plant is where the fungal toxin concentrates; if you prevent the plant from flowering, you decrease the concentration of the toxin.

3. You can dilute the amount of toxin available to the mares by giving other forages or feeds during late-term pregnancy.

4. You can keep the mares off pasture prior to day 21 of gestation or after day 300 and feed them something else altogether. Avoiding the fescue during these times prevents the problems.

If your mare hasn't been able to avoid fungus-infected fescue and she does deliver a foal, problems with milk production in the mare can be seen. Fortunately, there are drugs like domperidone and reserpine available that can help develop the udder and stimulate milk production. You'll need to call your veterinarian out immediately if you see a problem.

DEVELOPMENTAL ORTHOPEDIC DISEASE

Developmental orthopedic disease (hereafter referred to as DOD) is a phrase used to describe a number of clinical problems that affect growing young horses. Conditions that get lumped together under the DOD heading include epiphysistis, osteochondrosis, angular limb deformities, hock bone collapse (juvenile bone spavin) and contracted tendons (flexural deformities).

Many different factors have been associated with the condition; nutrition is only one of a group of factors that also includes excessive exercise, hereditary factors and trauma. Although the other factors are certainly important, nutrition is one of those things that you can easily meddle with. Thus, most people immediately look to good nutrition as a way to try to do something to prevent the condition. Two particular areas of the growing horse's diet get a lot of attention.

First is energy. Often, DOD is seen in horses that are growing big and getting there quickly. Big baby horses have a higher body weight, which may mean that they can more easily damage their young, soft cartilage. According to another theory, the rapidly growing bones may also outpace the growth of the tendons, leading to babies that are unable to straighten their legs due to contracted tendons. High levels of carbohydrate intake in young horses have been associated with DOD. Unfortunately, for those of you who like black-and-white answers, some other studies have failed to show any orthopedic problems in rapidly growing foals. Still, it is generally recommended that extremely rapid growth rates or growth spurts caused by inconsistent levels of nutrition should be avoided in young horses.

If, in the process of worrying about too rapid growth in your young horses, you overreact and end up starving them, that's not good either. If you severely restrict the amount of energy that a young horse gets, you can very effectively limit his growth and end up with a much smaller horse than you had hoped for. Although a horse with developmental orthopedic problems is not desirable, neither is is a rough-coated midget.

Mineral imbalances are the other big area of nutritional concern in DOD. Poorly balanced diets that are low in calcium, high in phosphorus, low in copper or high in zinc have all been related to problems in cartilage formation and bone mineralization (the process that makes bones hard). There are many complex interrelationships between the various minerals (that are much too tedious to mention here), but it's hardly controversial to assert that a growing horse's diet should be adequately supplied in minerals and that the minerals should be properly balanced.

CHAPTER 11

Feed Myths

GIVEN THAT EVERYONE WHO OWNS A HORSE HAS TO FEED it, it should probably come as no surprise that everyone also has an opinion about the best way to do so. Overlooking the fact that there's always more than one way to do most things, many well-meaning horse people come up with certain well-intentioned but somewhat inaccurate information about what you should and shouldn't do about feeding horses. These myths are apparently some sort of combination of observation, history, fact and old wives' tales (although, admittedly, some of those old wives *are* pretty sharp). At any rate, since you are going to have to feed your horse, you are also going to have to put up with these myths. Armed with the facts in the preceding chapters and the "myth-busting" information in this one, you should at least have a fighting chance at dispelling some of the misinformation that will confront you!

BRAN

Wheat bran has found a niche in equine feeding lore as a treatment or preventative for colic (abdominal pain). While it's not at all clear how bran has reached such an elevated status, it's reasonable to think that it may be due to an extension of the benefits of bran in the human diet. Nutritional research trumpets the benefits of fiber in the human diet in keeping people "regular"; bran is a pretty good source of fiber. Of course, fiber is good and necessary for horses, too—but it would be pretty hard to come up with a diet that's more fibrous than hay!

One of the reasons people feed bran to horses is in an apparent attempt to keep the horse's manure moist, in hopes that it might not get stuck along the way. Studies have been done evaluating the effects of large amounts of bran in a horse's diet. These studies showed that a diet of up to 50 percent bran doesn't change the amount of water in the horse's manure. Thus, if you're trying to keep a horse's manure a little looser by feeding him bran, you're really just wasting your time.

What about adding water to bran to make a "mash"? If you feed bran on a routine basis, soaking the bran doesn't help the horse digest it any better. If you feed a wet bran mash in hopes that it may get a little bit of water into the horse, it might, but an average horse needs at least five gallons of water a day. The quart or two that you use to make a bran mash isn't going to make much difference in the overall scheme of things. If your horse is colicking, a wet bran mash may get a little water into the system, but there are other, more effective ways to do that, too (such as a nasogastric tube, wielded by your veterinarian). Finally, it may be reasonable if you take the fact that your horse eats a wet bran mash as a sign that the horse is getting better. However, any other feed your horse likes would probably work just as well. About the only reason to feed bran wet is so that the stuff, which is normally pretty dry and flaky, doesn't blow around and get up the horse's nose.

Some people feed warm bran mashes to horses in an effort to raise their body temperature when it's cold outside. This is pretty silly. Due to their large volume and the relatively small, well-insulated surface area from which they lose body heat, horses have a difficult time ever getting cold. (The problem with horses is that they can't get rid of heat. Haven't you ever noticed how good your horse feels when it's cold outside?) The water you use to make the bran mash warm is going to cool off pretty quickly, anyway. (If you really want to make your horse warmer, feed him more hay. It's been shown that the heat produced by the digestion of five pounds of extra hay will increase the horse's core body temperature by over 1 degree Fahrenheit for almost four hours).

Bran isn't *bad* for horses (see the section on enteroliths, which follows); it's just not all that great for them. If your horse likes to have a bran mash from time to time and you enjoy preparing it, why not? There's certainly nothing bad that can be said about trying to reinforce the bond between horse and owner by feeding bran. Just don't put too much stock in it.

ALFALFA HAY AND THE KIDNEYS

For some odd reason, alfalfa hay has the reputation of being hard on a horse's kidneys. Presumably, this is because horses that eat lots of alfalfa hay tend to urinate a lot. There's a reason for this; alfalfa hay contains a lot of protein. Nitrogen is an element found in high quantities in protein. The body removes nitrogen through the kidneys, so if you feed a horse a lot of protein (from whatever the source, alfalfa hay or otherwise), you will most likely notice that it urinates a lot.

Producing urine is what the kidneys do. Producing extra urine doesn't wear out the kidneys any more than getting frequent haircuts wears out your hair. Paradoxically, some people have even argued that alfalfa hay is good for the kidneys because the extra urination helps flush out the horse's system. (It doesn't do that, either.)

CORN AND OATS ARE "HOT" FEEDS

Depending on your definition of *hot*, this myth can be interpreted in a couple of ways.

Some people use *hot* to refer to the horse's temperament; to them, a hot horse is excitable or energetic. To the extent that adding grain to a horse's diet provides extra energy needed for things like optimum performance, a horse that receives large amounts of these (or any) grains could potentially feel more energetic, especially because he is also fit and in optimum condition. In this instance, the word *hot* might also be a synonym for the word *normal*. Grains do cause a brief rise in blood sugar levels after they are eaten, and there has been some suggestion that this is associated with a more energetic demeanor. However, if you continue to feed grains in amounts that are greater than those needed to supply your horse's energy requirements, your hot horse will fairly quickly become a fat horse. Your other alternative is to *not* supply your horse enough dietary energy to meet its needs; while it may be somewhat less energetic as a result, you may have to deal with the humane society at some point.

The other definition of *hot* refers to the amount of internal heat produced as a result of the digestive process. Higher fiber content produces more internal heat. Thus, when compared to things like hay, corn and oats are actually much less of a *hot* feed.

Too Much Protein

Too much protein in the diet gets blamed for a number of medical problems in the horse, especially things like allergies and bumps in the skin. It's hard to figure out why this is the case; after all, there aren't any reports in the veterinary literature of "too much protein" disease. Nonetheless, it's a pervasive myth that protein in excess of dietary requirements can be harmful to a horse's health.

Certainly an adult horse doesn't *need* large amounts of protein in its diet. As you know, extra protein is just used for energy. It's not even particularly unnatural for a horse to consume excess protein in its diet. Grass pastures (the feed that horses evolved on) can have protein levels

· FIGURE 7 ·

of up to 26 percent in the spring, and horses seem to handle that just fine. The whole thing is just silly.

Even though there's no reason to believe that excessive protein in the diet is harmful in any way to a horse, diets with more than 20 percent protein have been correlated with slow race times. Furthermore, as with corn and oats, some people also assert that too much protein in the diet will make a horse *hot* (people are always looking for something or someone to blame for their problems). To the extent that extra protein is used for extra energy, the horse may develop of bit of an energetic ("hot") attitude with extra protein, but that's about it. (Of course, if you persist in overfeeding your horse, the biggest problem that you'll eventually have is getting your legs around it.)

While it's a waste of money to feed excessive levels of protein and it is certainly metabolically inefficient, it doesn't hurt your horse a bit.

PELLETS AND CUBES CAUSE HORSES TO CHOKE

Although many horses are able to exist happily on pelleted or cubed hay, there is a pervading belief that these processed hays are inherently dangerous to horses. That is, many people feel that horses fed hay cubes or pellets will choke on them.

Choke refers to an obstruction in the horse's esophagus (the tube that connects the mouth to the stomach). Anything that gets stuck in the esophagus prevents the passage of food and saliva into the stomach. Since the food and saliva can't go down, they come back out through the nostrils. Thus, any time you see a frantic horse with feed-colored saliva pouring out its nose, you can suspect that it's choking.

There's not any scientific evidence to back the commonly held belief that cubes and pellets contribute to the problem of choke, as long as horses eat in a normal fashion. If horses are aggressive eaters and bolt their pelleted or cubed feed, the chance that they could choke on it probably goes up. Thus, the problem is not specifically related to pellets and cubes; rather, it's related to the pig masquerading in horse clothing.

If you are going to feed pellets or cubes to your horse (for the many reasons why you might, refer to chapters 5 and 10), it might make some sense to try to slow down how quickly your horse can eat them. Here are a few tricks that might help:

- Make sure that the teeth are in good shape so that the horse can chew the feed before swallowing it.
- Introduce pellets slowly into the diet; mix pellets into the current feed in gradually increasing amounts while slowly decreasing the amount of the old feed.
- Gradually introduce any changes in pellet size.
- Water down the pellets before you feed them.
- Add oil to the pellets before you feed them.
- Have fresh water available while the horse eats.
- Put the horse's feed on the ground. Horses normally eat from the ground; feeding them with their head up in the air increases the bend in the neck and is sort of like asking a person to eat with his or her chin on her chest.
- Feed in large, shallow pans so that the feed is in a thin layer and the horse can't get a big mouthful of it.
- Put large rocks or bricks in the feeder to make the horse pick the feed from around them.

CRIMPED OATS ARE BETTER THAN WHOLE OATS

Many horse people won't feed whole oats to horses. They want to feed oats that have been crimped or flaked in hopes that the horse will be able to get more nutrition out of the processed grains. Research indicates that horses do get more nutrition from crimped oats, but it's only about 6 percent more. That's certainly not enough difference to pay a premium.

HORSES EAT THINGS BECAUSE THEY ARE LACKING SOMETHING

Horses will eat just about anything. They do not eat vitamins or minerals (or anything else) according to what they need, however, with the single exception of sodium, which is one of the two elements that make up salt (of course, your horse will not become sodium deficient if you give him *anything* to eat). Ponies fed diets that are lacking in calcium (in experimental situations) do not develop a liking for supplements that contain calcium. If they are allowed to consume vitamins and minerals in unlimited amounts, horses will eat different amounts—but not according to what they need.

The eating of stuff that horses don't normally eat is called *pica*. This sort of behavior can be perfectly normal. Horses eat dirt and everything else for a number of reasons, including boredom, taste preferences and trying to give their owners something else to worry about. Horses that are lacking in critical vitamins and minerals may also start happily eating mouthfuls of dirt or other unusual substances. Horses that are fed experimental diets low in fiber turn into wood-chewing beavers or begin to graze contentedly on their manure (if your horse eats hay it will not lack fiber, however). Thus, if your horse really seems to be eating lots of stuff that it normally wouldn't, it may not mean that there's a problem, but it may be worth getting his diet looked into, if only for your piece of mind.

New Hay Must Cure Before Being Fed

Some people think that new hay must cure in the barn before it can be fed. No. You can feed properly dried and baled hay as soon as it's out of the field.

However, if hay is baled when it is too moist, changes in the hay will indeed occur, so waiting for the hay to "cure" won't help any. Freshly cut plant material is still metabolically active; if hay is too moist when it is baled, heat will be produced. That heat can be enough to cause spontaneous combustion of the hay (and the barn that holds it)! Of course, hay that is too wet will also mold, and that's no good either.

First-Cutting Hay Isn't Any Good

For some reason, some people think that the first seasonal cutting of hay is often inferior to the cuttings that follow. It's as if the plant has to figure out how to be nutritious; sort of like a nutritional mulligan. It's true that if the hay producer lets a lot of weeds grow up in the fields or lets the hay get too mature before cutting it, the hay won't be of good quality. But this is a problem with the producer, not the hay. Good-quality hay is good-quality hay, whatever the cutting.

Hay Bellies

Did you ever see a horse with a prominent abdomen and hear it described as a having a "hay belly"? That colorful term is based on the mistaken conclusion that feeding a horse too much hay will give the horse a pendulous abdomen. When you look at most horses with hay bellies, you'll actually find that most of them are *under* weight and in poor condition. If your horse is a little thin with a big belly, you should be working on developing an improved exercise program to tighten up those muscles and on a balanced feeding program rather than cutting back on its hay.

HIGH-ENERGY FEEDS THAT DON'T GET HORSES "HIGH"

People are always looking for feeds to give horses more energy without having the horses act more energetic. This is pretty much impossible. To the extent that adding fat to a horse's diet may help keep the blood sugar levels down, you can try to add fat to your horse's diet to give it more energy. However, if you are going to exercise your horse and keep it fit and if you are going to feed it properly, then you are going to have a horse that feels good. The word to describe this set of circumstances is *normal*.

COASTAL BERMUDA HAY CAUSES COLIC

Some myths have an element of truth in them. There's no question that many horses in the southern United States are fed coastal Bermuda grass hay and that these horses do just great on it. However, there's also no question that there are reports of an increased incidence of impaction-type colics in horses that are fed this hay. What's going on here?

The problem is most likely related to the maturity of the hay, not to the hay itself. If coastal Bermuda grass is allowed to mature before it is cut, the resulting hay is coarse and difficult for the horse to digest. Hay that is poorly digestible isn't broken down as easily by the bacteria of the horse's hindgut. Thus, instead of digestible bits of plant fiber that can easily exit the horse's intestine, it's possible that large bits of fiber can accumulate and stick together, forming something of a straw mat inside the intestine. The resulting plug causes the signs of colic.

Once again, the question is a matter of feed quality. This book has consistently stressed the importance of good-quality feed for the horse. The "coastal Bermuda hay and colic" myth is another good opportunity to stress it again.

FEEDING OIL TO PREVENT COLIC

Some people dose their horses with oil on a regular basis in the forlorn hope that it will help prevent a colic. Presumably, the reason they do this is that when horses are treated for colic it's a fairly common practice to administer a good quantity of light mineral oil to act as a lubricant or laxative. However, administering mineral oil prior to a colic does nothing to prevent its occurrence.

If you use another type of oil, such as corn or linseed oil, in an effort to prevent colic, you're *really* wasting your time. Corn oil is almost completely digested by the horse and doesn't make it all the way down the digestive tract. Giving plant oils to horses will increase the energy level of their diet but won't help prevent colic.

VINEGAR, MINERALS, ALFALFA AND ENTEROLITHS

Enteroliths are hard, round "stones" that form in the horse's large intestine. They form much as a pearl forms inside an oyster, in layers of mineral material. Stones don't cause any problems in the horse's gut until they get too big; then, they can plug up the intestinal tract and cause a colic that requires surgery to correct.

As a point in fact, no one knows why horses develop enteroliths. (It has been observed that they occur more often in Arabian horses than in other breeds.) Yet that hasn't stopped people from trying to come up with ways to solve the problem (apparently following the time-honored tradition of, "If you don't know, guess"). There's as yet no scientific basis for believing any of the following proposed solutions to the problem of enteroliths:

- Vinegar in the feed. It has been well demonstrated that adding a cup of cider vinegar to a horse's diet will make its intestinal environment more acidic. According to one theory, an acidic intestine is supposed to lead to the formation of fewer stones. This idea is based on nutritional therapy for dogs that develop mineral stones in their bladders. Making the urine more acidic by feeding things such as ammonium chloride does help decrease the formation of bladder stones in dogs. To date, no one has ever demonstrated that feeding vinegar to horses to make the intestines more acidic will decrease the formation of enteroliths, or even that an intestinal environment that's not acidic enough will cause the formation of stones.

- Alfalfa gets blamed for cases of stone formation (much as it gets blamed for just about everything else). That's most likely because both alfalfa hay and enteroliths are high in calcium. There's no proven link between the two.

- Wheat bran gets fingered as a potential stone-forming agent because it has a high phosphorus content and it may make the environment in the intestines less acidic. Even though bran is not particularly great for horses (as noted earlier) it's not particularly bad, either.

- The mineral content in the water gets blamed for stones, too. While the water in some areas is relatively high in minerals, it's a pretty big leap of faith to believe that it also causes enteroliths. Besides, when faced with water that has a high mineral content, your choices are fairly limited and include such inconvenient choices as processing the horse's water to remove minerals or moving.

The reasons that some horses form stones in their intestines are not currently known. As much as you would like to have an easy solution to the problem, unfortunately, there isn't one.

Epilogue

Thᴀᴛ's ɪᴛ. Rᴇᴀʟʟʏ. Fᴇᴇᴅɪɴɢ ᴀ ʜᴏʀsᴇ ɪs ɴᴏᴛ ᴛʜᴀᴛ ʜᴀʀᴅ. It's important but not all that difficult.

Start by learning what's available to feed to horses in your area. Continue by finding out what's in the feed. Sit down and think about the nutritional demands you make of your horse, and then supply the feed or feeds to fill those needs. That's it!

The thing to keep in mind is that horses are kept and fed all over the world. Depending on where the horses live, they may be fed different things. Thus, although the "best" and "only" way to feed a horse might make lots of sense to you and your neighbor, it might bring a smile to someone on the other side of the globe who uses a completely different (and completely effective) feeding program for their horse. There truly is more than one way to get your horse properly fed.

The most important thing is to get concepts like "good" and "bad" out of the discussion of feeding a horse. Feed has no inherent moral qualities. Good and bad aren't the issues; the proper quality and quantities are. Feed is all made up of the same things. Your job is to try to figure out what those things are and how to get them into your horse. Leave the moralizing to other folks.

Index

A

A&M, 39

Additives, hay, 51

Alfalfa, 27, 35–36, 90, 101, 104, 133, 142

Alfalfa meal, 39

Amino acid, 6, 22, 24, 25, 56, 62

Angular limb deformities, 129

Animal fat, 5

Ash, 11

B

Babies, feeding, 102–103

Bacteria

    intestinal, 20, 23, 24, 26, 27, 29

    supplemental, 71–72

Bahia grass, 38

Barley, 41, 44, 53

Barley hay. *See* cereal grain hay

Barrel-racing horses, feeding, 110–111

Beet pulp, 44, 119

Bermuda grass, 38

"Big head," 45, 68

Biotin, 10, 66

Bird's foot trefoil, 36

Blister beetle, 118

Blood flow, to GI tract, 23

Blood sugar, 24, 108–109

Bluegrass, 36

Body condition, 86–89

Botulism, 51, 52

Bran, 42, 44–45, 119, 131–133, 142

Bread, 46

Brewer's dried grains, 43

Bromegrass, 36

Broodmare, feeding, 96, 117

C

Calcium, 12, 28, 35, 67–68, 101, 123

Calories, in feed, 1–2, 61

Canola oil, 5

Canola meal, 43, 101

Cantharidin toxicosis, 118

Carbohydrates, 2–3, 22, 24–25, 109, 129

    nonstructural, 3, 25

    structural, 2–3, 24–25, 33

Carnitine, 75–76

Carrots, 46

Cereal grain hay, 35, 38, 90

Chaff, 39, 93

Chemical, digestive, 20, 21

Choke, 53, 136–137

Chondroitin sulfate, 77

Chromium, 73–74, 127

Chronic obstructive pulmonary disease, 123

Clover, 36

Coastal bermuda grass, 38, 140–141

Coconut, 47

Coenzyme Q10, 76

Colic, 16, 26, 40, 84, 89, 115–120, 140–141

Colic surgery, feeding after, 118–120

Contracted tendons, 129

Copper, 13–14, 68, 102

Corn, 5, 40, 44, 53, 56, 133–134

Corn oil, 5, 46

Cottonseed meal, 43

Cracking, 55

Creatine, 76

Creep feeding, 103

Crimping, 55

Cubes. *See* hay cubes

Cyanocolbolamin, 9, 66

D

DMG, 74

Dates, 47

Deficiencies, eating and, 138

Developmental orthopedic disease, 104, 128–130

Digestion, 19–23

Duodenum, 22

Dust, and hay, 51–52, 81, 123

E

EMN, 124

EPM, 66, 124–126

Electrolyte, 13, 23, 62, 69–70, 113

Endurance horse, 113

Energy, in feed, 1–3, 24, 61, 81–82, 100

Enteroliths, 45, 141–143

Enzymes

digestive, 20, 21

supplemental, 72

Epiphysitis, 129

Equine polysaccharide storage
myopathy, 127

Esophagus, 22

Exercise, 63, 90–91

Extruded feeds, 57–58, 59

F

Fat

body, 26, 27, 89–90

dietary, 5, 27, 91, 108, 109–100,
119

Fatty acids, 22, 23, 27

Feed quality, 58–59, 81

Feeding

changes, 116

frequency, 29–30, 116

guidelines, 81–84

timing, 108–109

Fermentation, 20, 21, 23

Fescue, 37, 127–128

Feterita, 41

Fiber, 23, 24, 33, 41, 70, 71,
92, 138

Flaking, 55

Flat-track horses, 110–111

Folic acid, 10, 125

Forage, 29, 81

Foregut, 22

G

Gas, 21

Ghee, 47

Glucosamine, 77

Glucose, 24

Glycogen, 26

Grain, 3, 26, 39–40, 53–56,
59, 91

processing, 53–54

Grain sorghum, 41

Grass hay, 3, 35, 36–38

Green chop, 33–34

Grinding, 55

Growth, 99–102

H

HYPP, 121–122

Hay, 3, 11, 34–35, 50–52, 58–59

bellies, 139–140

dust and mold in, 51–52

new, 139

Haylage, 39, 52, 123

Hay cubes, 52–53, 93, 117,
136–137

Hegari, 41

Herbs, 72–73

"High" horses, 110, 140

Hominy, 40

Honey, 47

"Hot" feeds, 113–134

Hydroxymethyl butyrate (HMB), 75–76

I

Ileum, 22

Iodine, 14, 28

Impaction, 116, 117, 118, 119

Insulin, 24, 73, 108, 110

Iron, 14

J–K

Jaggery, 47

Jejunum, 22

Juvenile bone spavin, 129

Kidney, 7, 92, 126
  and alfalfa hay, 133
  disease, 123

L

Lactation, feeding, 63–, 97–99

Lactic acid, 25, 117

Laminitis, 26, 40, 89, 120–121

Lawn trimmings, 34

Lespedeza, 36

Legume hay, 34–35, 67

Linseed meal, 43

Lipoma, 89

Liver, 22, 27, 90, 92
  disease, 122

Lucerne hay, 35, 47. *See also* alfalfa

M

Macromineral, 12–13

Magnesium, 12

Maintenance, feeding for, 85–86

Maize, 40. *See also* Corn

Manganese, 14, 102

Micromineral, 13–14

Milk, feed and quality of, 99

Milo, 41, 53

Minerals, 11–13, 22, 28, 55–56, 61–69, 101, 102, 130, 142–143
  chelated, 15

Molasses, 44, 56, 59

Mold, and hay, 51, 81, 116

Monensin, 118

N

Niacin, 10

Nitrogen, 6, 27, 133

Nutraceutical, 77

O

O&M, 39

Oat hay. *See* cereal grain hay

Oats, 5, 40–41, 53, 56, 133–134, 137–138

Octocosanol, 76–77

Oil, and colic, 141

Older horses, 91–94

Orchardgrass, 36

Osteochondrosis, 68, 129

P

Pancreas, 22

Pangola grass, 38

Pantothenic acid, 9

Parasites, 32, 90, 102

Pasture, 3, 31–33, 124

Pellets, 56–57, 93, 117, 136–137

Performance horse feeding,
    107–113

Phosphorus, 12, 28, 35, 68, 92,
    101

Pica, 138

Pituitary tumors, 92

Polo horses, feeding, 110–111

Potassium, 122

Potatoes, 46

Pregnancy, feeding, 63, 96–97

Protein, 5–7, 26–27, 63–64, 92,
    100–101, 123
       supplements, 42–43

R

Rape, 43

Rectum, 23

Reed canarygrass, 37

Respiratory disease, 123

Rhabdomyolysis, 74, 126–127

Riboflavin, 9

Rice bran, 45

Rickets, 67

Rolling, 55

Round bales, 51

Ruminant, 20

Rye, 41–42

Ryegrass, 36–37

S

Saliva, 21–22, 23

Sand colic, 118

Salt, 11

Selenium, 14, 28, 69, 127

"Senior" horses. *See* older horses

Show horses, 111

Silage, 39, 52, 123

Small intestine, 22

Solumycin, 118

Sorghum. *See* grain sorghum

Soybean meal, 43, 56, 101

Soybean oil, 5

Stallion, feeding, 95–96

Starch, 3, 22, 25, 26, 29, 40, 58,
    108

Stomach, 22

Stones, intestinal, 45, 141–143

Straw, 38–39

Sugarcane, 46

Sugars, 3, 22

Sulfur, 13

Sunflowers, 47

Supplements, 61–77

"Sweet" feed, 56, 117

T

Teeth, 21, 90, 93

Thiamine, 9, 66

Thin horse, 90–91

Thyroid gland, 28

Timothy, 36

Torsion, 117

Trace mineral, 11, 69

Tying up. *See* rhabdomyolysis

V

Vegetable oil, 46

Vinegar, 142

Vitamin, 8–11, 28, 55–56, 61–69

    A, 8, 9, 22, 28, 40, 65, 95

    B, 8, 9, 66, 122

    B1, 9, 66

    B2, 9

    B3, 9

    B6, 9

    B12, 9, 66

    C, 8, 10, 67

    D, 8, 10, 22, 28, 67

    E, 8, 10, 22, 28, 67, 95–96, 124, 127

    fat soluble, 8, 28

    K, 8, 10, 28, 67

    water soluble, 8, 28

W

Water, 15, 23, 28–29, 70, 81, 116

Weanlings, feeding, 103–104

Weight. *See also* body condition

    estimation of, 80, 82–83

    gain, 91

    of feed, 80–81

    overweight, 89–90

    underweight, 90–91, 92

Wheat

    bran, 42, 44–45. *See also* bran

    hay. *See* cereal grain hay

    middlings, 42

    mill run, 42

Y–Z

Yearlings, feeding, 104–105

Yeast, 70–71, 92

Zinc, 14, 68–69, 102